Cape May Point

Three Walking Tours of Historic Cottages

Joe J. Jordan

4880 Lower Valley Road, Atglen, PA 19310 USA

DEDICATION
For Sarah.

Cover photo by Don Touzeau
Author's Portrait by Hugh Hales-Tooke
Designed by John P. Cheek
Cover Design by John P. Cheek
Type set in Carleton/Humanist 521 BT

ISBN: 0-7643-2108-0
Printed in China

Published by Schiffer Publishing Ltd.
4880 Lower Valley Road
Atglen, PA 19310
Phone: (610) 593-1777; Fax: (610) 593-2002
E-mail: Info@schifferbooks.com

For the largest selection of fine reference books on this and related subjects, please visit our web site at **www.schifferbooks.com**
We are always looking for people to write books on new and related subjects. If you have an idea for a book please contact us at the above address.

This book may be purchased from the publisher.
Include $3.95 for shipping.
Please try your bookstore first.
You may write for a free catalog.

In Europe, Schiffer books are distributed by
Bushwood Books
6 Marksbury Ave.
Kew Gardens
Surrey TW9 4JF England
Phone: 44 (0) 20 8392-8585; Fax: 44 (0) 20 8392-9876
E-mail: info@bushwoodbooks.co.uk
Free postage in the U.K., Europe; air mail at cost.

Contents

Acknowledgments 4

Introduction 5

Part 1 – Sea Grove and Cape May Point 6

Part 2 – The Survivors – Three Walking Tours 17

Tour 1 – Along Cape Avenue 17
Tour 2 – Along the Oceanside 42
Tour 3 – Along the Bay Shore 80

Part 3 – The Departed – Two Dozen Rare Photographs 101

Part 4 – The New Arrivals –Ten "Top-Picks" Contemporary Homes 114

Appendix: Glossary 134
            Illustrated Glossary 136

Index 140

ACKNOWLEDGMENTS

I wish to thank the dozens of homeowners who have reviewed my descriptions of their properties and have offered constructive suggestions, corrections, photographs, or additional information not available from public records.

Thank you Trudy Cohen, Nick DeCredico, and Neal Blank. Without the thoughtful offering of your professional photographic equipment there would be no color pictures to illustrate this book.

I am especially grateful to Carol Rauch for your thorough and creative editing of the final manuscript. I appreciate the lengthy conversations I have had with David Rutherford about the early cottages. These have been very helpful thanks to his astonishing memory.

To the following I am indebted for your generous donation of photographs: Don Touzeau, Lewis Tanner, Suzanne Benoit, Margaret Killian, Sally Sachs, and Andrea Moffatt. The Cape May County Historical Society must also be credited for permitting the inclusion of many of their historic photographs.

Finally, I'm obliged to these five local architects who joined me in identifying those contemporary houses we felt should be included on the tours: Bob Cassway, Gabrielle Larkin, Bob Mazille, Jerry Roller, and Joe Salerno.

INTRODUCTION

For the vacationing visitor, this book will be your guide for three delightful walking tours of Cape May Point's historic buildings – all from the nineteenth century.

For the Cape May Point resident, it will be a ready reference to the seventy authentic cottages and chapels that can be found on almost every block of the early Sea Grove community.

The book is arranged in four parts. Part I outlines the first quarter-century of Sea Grove and Cape May Point. A reading of this brief history will add to the enjoyment of each tour and answer many questions for those less familiar with this unique shore resort.

The second part provides a choice of three self-guided tours – all designed for a leisurely stroll of an hour or so. The number-keyed street map makes each route easy to follow. All start at the foot of Cape Avenue and head north, east, or west.

The third part illustrates many of the houses that that did not survive the raging storms that have devoured one-fifth of the original community.

The last part focuses on ten of the most delightful new homes that have been built here over the past several decades. They represent the "top picks" of six architects who make the Point their home.

The appendix contains an illustrated glossary and a convenient index of important names, places, and organizations that appear in the text in boldface type.

Where house names appear in italics it indicates the name of the current owner or its common name, and not that of the original owner.

Because no tax records from 1875 to 1900 exist today, precise dates for the construction of each building are seldom possible to come by. The author, therefore, has used *circa* to indicate the probable date based on available deed records.

Part I

CAPE MAY POINT AND SEA GROVE

From the beginning of the nineteenth century **Cape May** was *the* shore resort for Philadelphia, Baltimore, and Washington. Until the 1860s there was no alternative resort in South Jersey. Before the railroads arrived Cape May had offered easy access down the Delaware Bay – first by schooner and then by steamship.

The city soon had boundless sybaritic pleasures to offer eager vacationers. There were, however, those who recoiled from the worldly behavior to be found there. They were dismayed by the disrespect for the Sabbath, or by excessive gambling and public drunkenness.

THE FOUNDER

Alexander Whilldin was such a person. He was a religious man, a deeply committed Presbyterian. Though born in Philadelphia, Whilldin came from an old Cape May County family. He grew up near **Cape May Court House** on the homestead farm, but at the age of sixteen, he returned to Philadelphia to pursue a life in commerce. It was a very successful life. For fifty years, each summer season found Whilldin escaping from business for relaxing sojourns in Cape May. He observed "with regret, the increase of a bad fashion which renders the season for rest and health-giving resort to nature but a wearying round of dissipation."

During these visits, Whilldin thought about a different kind of place – perhaps not a fundamentally religious community like **Ocean Grove**, New Jersey, but a place, that in his words, would become a "moral and religious seaside home." Fortunately, Alexander Whilldin had the means to achieve his mission. He owned all the land that was to become **Sea Grove**! His wife of almost forty years was a **Stites**, and the property had been in her family since 1712. Now nearing seventy, Whilldin decided to act. With the agreement of his wife, Jane, with whom he said, "they had laid the matter before God," he took the first decisive step with the formation of the **West Cape May Land Company** in 1872, and The **Sea Grove Association** in 1875.

WHILLDIN'S ASSOCIATES

In addition to Alexander Whilldin, two other Philadelphians, retail merchant **John Wanamaker**, and architect **James C. Sidney**, were to have a powerful influence on the development of Sea Grove. Whilldin provided Sea Grove's foundation; with his vision and his property; the influential Wanamaker contributed to its fame; and the talented Sidney supplied this new seaside resort with its enduring form.

STITES BEACH

Today, it's hard to imagine the wild place that **Cape May Point** was in 1875. At that time it was just a wilderness known as **Stites Beach**, or **Barren Beach**. Fifteen-foot dunes lined the beaches. Further back were the pin oaks, pitch pines, holly, and sassafras. The local newspaper, *Star of the Cape*, called it "…a desert wilderness of trees, brush, brambles, and sand," and "a dense growth of timber, woody copse, and briar tangles, with a sea front of sand hills and inhabited by rabbits and other wild game."

THE SEA GROVE ASSOCIATION

Such was the site that Alexander Whilldin decided to develop as a new seaside resort. With the presentation of an application to the New Jersey legislature for a charter of incorporation under the name of the **Sea Grove Association**, Whilldin set out to develop the family tract into a Christian resort. The formation of the Sea Grove Association provided the legal right to create a new community under New Jersey law. Long before that action was taken, the serious planning had been underway. **James C. Sidney**, an English immigrant whose practice was in Philadelphia, had already been engaged as the architect. Sidney had gained knowledge in civil engineering, landscape planning, surveying, and map-making, putting it to good use in his plans for Sea Grove.

SIDNEY'S PLAN

After he had leveled the protective dunes that had lined the shore for centuries, Sidney replaced them with timber bulkheads and jetties as a means of retarding erosion This was a fateful error. By the 1960s, the sea had claimed twenty percent of the town – all of the streets and houses along the shoreline. The dunes we see today were artificially created in 1968, but are now a more formidable barrier to erosion than the natural dunes of the past.

The most striking characteristic of Sidney's town plan was the **Pavilion Circle**, a large, round park. In its center Sidney placed the impressive open-air **Pavilion** where 1,500 people could worship. This arrangement announced loud and clear that this was the heart and soul of the community, a Christian community with public worship as its cornerstone.

The 261-acre site was to provide a total of 981 building lots. Most were at least 5,000 square feet in area. The land was undulating, with some sections as much as 25-feet above sea level, but the lower land between the lake and the ocean was filled, and the final street pattern emerged relatively level.

No Streets

To assure visitors of the prominence of this new community, there were to be no *streets*, only *avenues* (with but two exceptions: Surf Street, probably because it was to be used as a service drive to the **Sea Grove House Hotel**, and Lake Drive). The three main thoroughfares, Cape, Ocean, and Central, radiated out from the **Pavilion Park** like the spokes of a wheel.

The street plan was quite logical. Cape Avenue was its "Main Street" because it was the point of entry from the **Cape Island Turnpike** (now Sunset Boulevard). The turnpike brought in visitors from the **Steamship Landing** on the bay, or from the **Railroad Depot** in Cape May. Cape Avenue extended from the turnpike to the point of land where ocean and bay intersected and where the first hotel, the **Sea Grove House**, was located.

The other two radial streets also terminated at the shoreline; Ocean Avenue, running north south, ended at the ocean beach, while Central Avenue, running east west, terminated at the bay beach. Another prominent road, Beach Avenue, ran along the shoreline to provide beachfront lots where the wealthy could build their impressive summer homes.

Lighthouse Avenue became the perimeter-street to the east, and Alexander Avenue became its counterpart to the west. Another feature road was Lake Drive, completely encircling **Lake Lily** and offering a pleasant track where *nouveau-riche* drivers could display their fine livery. Interspersed among these key roads was a rectangular grid of residential streets. Some of these are gone today, victims of the northeast storms and hurricanes that severely eroded the shoreline. Those that remain bear their original names.

Consider the ones between Cape and Central Avenue named for precious stones: Diamond, Emerald, Crystal, and Pearl. Between Central and Alexander, prominent Presbyterian ministers were honored: Brainard, Knox, and Alexander. From Cape to Lighthouse, celebrated universities appear: Harvard, Yale, Princeton, Cambridge and Oxford. In the quadrant farthest from the shore (and since less valuable for development, it remained in its wild wooded state the longest) are the streets appropriately named for the dominant trees to be found there: Cedar, Holly, and Oak. It's hardly surprising that the names of the founding families were included – **Whilldin** and **Stites** Avenues.

Spiritual Caretakers

The Sea Grove Association encouraged the ministry to settle in and ensure the spiritual purity of the community by offering them free lots – the only stipulation was that they build a house within a year. The ministers responded – Protestant clergy built ten percent of the first cottages. **Rev. Adolph Spaeth** was able to build the beautiful Rosemere Cottage on Yale Avenue for $1,100. Many two-story cottages with three bedrooms were being put up for a similar amount. Ownership of several lots by the ministers was common enough, with **Rev. W. R. Stockton**, an Episcopalian, acquiring the most. And so Sea Grove's religious foundation was assured, and the ministers profited handsomely.

EARLY PROGRESS?

It appears that the two local newspapers, the *Cape May Ocean Wave* and the *Star of the Cape*, were regularly being fed information on the real estate sales at the new resort; what we would call today "news releases." Each paper reported what it was told, so the picture we have from that time may be a rosier one than investigative reporting would have produced. The newspapers were told that by March of 1875 ten lots were sold, by April almost sixty, by May another twenty-three, and by June, in time for the official opening, twenty-seven cottages had been built, and the total number of lots sold had zoomed to 225. That approaches a twenty-five percent sellout – not bad for the first six months' effort! However, two more years of marketing only added forty-four additional sales. From twenty-five percent sales in six months to only five percent sales over the next two years was a substantial letdown.

THE COTTAGES

Most of the early cottages were modest in size by today's standards. A few show-places, like the cottages of **Alexander Whilldin**, **John Wanamaker**, and **President Benjamin Harrison** were there for the wealthy. The typical three-bedroom house was often built in two months because the Point's early cottages were largely second homes for summer vacationers – they didn't have heat and air conditioning, electricity, gas, or phone. Bathrooms had a split personality – tub and sink inside, toilet in the outhouse. Kerosene was fuel for the lamps and cooking stove, ice was for the icebox.

Foundations for the model cottage were really simple. They typically consisted of brick piers set six to eight feet apart, instead of the continuous foundation wall so common today. The narrow piers even lacked spread footings since the sandy soil could easily support the light wood frame construction above. A heavy perimeter beam carried the stud frame of the exterior bearing walls. Room width was often limited to twelve feet, an economical span for the floor joists.

The outer walls had white cedar or white pine clapboard siding nailed directly to the studs. The interior finish was plaster on wood lath. Today we would add sheathing between the siding and studs, building paper, plus a vapor barrier and insulating material. Sub-floors were uncommon; most houses had random-width yellow pine boards nailed directly to the floor joists. The same applied to the roofs, which usually had a steep pitch, but again, no sheathing boards on the rafters. The hand-split cedar shingles made a first class roof with a life span of fifty to one hundred years.

The key man was the carpenter builder, who put together almost everything but the plastering and painting. Few cottages had an architect; most house plans and decorative details came from pattern books or from the skill and experience of the builder.

THE GARDENS

Today's interest in natural habitats and native plants was not the fashion in Sea Grove. The mission then was to tame the unruly wilderness into a more pristine setting for the vacationing gentry. Each property had its lawn and flowerbed, and a picket fence often staked out the property lines. Evidence of this remains today. Many of the houses along Cape, Ocean, and Central Avenues, from the beach to the circle, have kept their well-tended lawns, while those properties developed in more recent times have opted for the natural landscape, preserving what they found and adding plants native to the region. It is this variety, each authentic in its own way, which contributes much to the beguiling appeal of Cape May Point today.

THE SURVIVORS

Of the houses built over Sea Grove's first quarter-century, we are very fortunate that about seventy survive today. All of these are described and illustrated in **Part 2 – Three Walking Tours**. Those no longer with us were most often casualties of the advancing sea. However, many beachfront homes were moved to safer locations as the receding shoreline made their fate clear. Accurate information on which of these houses have been moved to their present location, as well as evidence of their original setting is scarce. Others have been claimed by fire, but with the exception of raging fires in 1888 and 1908, such losses have not been severe.

All of these buildings have been altered in some fashion over the years. Few have retained the cedar shingle roofs they started with, and most have replaced these with less costly asphalt shingles.

Unfortunately, when it came time to repaint, many owners chose instead to use the new aluminum siding or the old cement-asbestos shingles to cover the original clapboards. This change in siding texture from the narrower shadow lines of clapboard to the much wider and fainter lines of the shingles is aesthetically unfortunate.

RECOGNIZING THE ORIGINALS

One of the identifying characteristics of the early houses is the form of their double-hung windows. Almost all of these have a dividing mullion in the center of the top and bottom sashes, creating a distinctive window with four rectangular panes of glass. This style went out of fashion with the demise of the Victorian era.

Houses were often planned as simple rectangles with fairly steep gable roofs and deep eaves. Larger cottages added a wing for an el shape, or two wings in a cruciform plan. Virtually all had open verandas facing the street, some wrapping around the sides. Gingerbread was in fashion as the hallmark of the Victorian cottage. Its extensive design variations did much to create diversity of style among the early cottages.

Most of the open porches are now screened in – homage to our insect friends, including the ubiquitous mosquito and voracious fly. Others have been closed in to add an extra room. Still others have so many additions and alterations that it takes an experienced eye to imagine the original form.

CHANGING THE RULES

In 1984, the only Cape May Point store still in operation was **Harriet's General Store** at the northwest corner of Cape and Pavilion Avenues. That year, the local zoning ordinance had undergone many fundamental changes. The Point was to become a community of single-family dwellings. Existing uses that did not conform to the new purely-residential zoning were permitted to continue operating under a "grandfather clause." Harriet's and its successors would have no threat of competition from other stores.

COMMERCIAL DEMISE

Under the new zoning there would be no more stores, no more hotels, and no more boarding houses. These commercial enterprises had been the backbone of Sea Grove. Businesses that had been essential in its formative days lost their usefulness over time. By the first decade of the twentieth century all the hotels were gone. Before the start of WWII the boarding houses would also be gone, and so would all the little stores that had sprung to life season after season since Sea Grove first welcomed vacationers in 1875. From 1875 to 1900, thirty stores had opened, but not many survived for more than a few years

Cape Avenue could have been called "Main Street" because of the concentration of shops to be found there. No zoning code restricted or directed their location. They were most often opened in one of the two story cottages, although a few had been built as store buildings. In 1890, all five of Cape May Point's stores were to be found on Cape Avenue between the Pavilion Circle and Beach Avenue. Ten years later, at the turn of the century, Cape still had four of them, but now Yale and Ocean had each gained two, and Lincoln one. This was the Point's peak period of commercial development.

SOCIAL ACCOMMODATIONS

With the arrival of its second summer season in 1876, Sea Grove could offer visitors a choice of three hotels. The best accommodations were found at the **Sea Grove House**, followed by the **Cape House** and the **Centennial House**. The latter two resembled boarding houses more than hotels. Scarcely a block separated the three, all clustered along Cape Avenue close by the waterfront. What differentiated them were the extent of entertainment offered and the refinement of the accommodations provided. All three are gone today, victims of fire or the sea.

The drive for social status was very much alive in nineteenth century Cape May Point. What better way to establish one's position than membership in a club for one's equals (or betters)? A physician from Pittsburgh, **Dr. Randall T. Hazzard**, may have been dreaming such dreams. Why not build his own country club? On Lake drive at the corner of Central Avenue, at considerable expense, he converted an abandoned ice-house into **The Cape May Point Social Club**.

Announcing that its objective was "the advancement of social life in Cape May Point," it opened its doors on August 11, 1899 with (what else) a reception and tea. Determined to make the lake and the clubhouse the focal point of social life, Hazzard also built the famous **Rustic Bridge** overlooking the clumps of lily pads at the north end of the lake. The clubhouse remains, now a private residence, but the picturesque bridge is gone.

GOODBYE SEA GROVE

In 1878, just three years into its infancy, Sea Grove had a problem. It was with the Government of the United States. The feds determined that its post office that had been operating since March of 1876 wasn't kosher. After all, the Sea Grove Association was not a government body; it was a private enterprise, operating rather independently within the Township of Lower.

Facing up to this predicament, the Association successfully petitioned the State Legislature to incorporate as a borough, independent of Lower Township. The taxpayers approved this in an April referendum. Next problem – the postal service objected to the name Sea Grove. Some say they thought Sea Grove's mail would get mixed with **Ocean Grove's**, since the names were so similar. **Cape May Point** (a name certainly not to be confused with **Cape May City**!) was chosen and approved. So the Point has two birthdays – 1875 as Sea Grove and 1878 as Cape May Point.

DANGER SIGNS

Five years after that first birthday, building pace in Cape May Point was slowing to a halt. By 1880 the *Cape May Wave* observed, "while 1876 was a promising year, growth since then has not achieved expectations. A certain class affirms that it will never prosper as a temperance resort." The newspaper further reported on January 29: "As a seaside resort conducted on puritanical principles…Cape May Point appears to have reached the end of its string…There are people wicked enough who account for the failure of Cape May Point because of the strict temperance and anti-amusement provisions of its charter of incorporation. The directors were invested among other exclusive powers of regulation and control, to forbid the sale of intoxicating liquors, to require of property owners any style and character of improvements, etc., and the directors themselves ruled against allowing any place of amusement."

THE GREAT AUCTION

The tremors of 1880 foretold the calamity that struck in 1881. Bankruptcy arrived. A January audit showed the Sea Grove Association's net worth to be less than $30,000! The venture had been financed by a $60,000 mortgage loan with a five-year balloon. Final payment was now due – desperate measures were called for. The property had to be sold. As late as March the Association couldn't get their asking price and a public auction appeared to be the only solution.

Alexander Whilldin and the **Sea Grove Association** had to abandon their dream. All restrictions that had been placed on building lots would be lifted. No longer would a purchaser have to build within three years; a speculator could hold the land indefinitely. Cottage plans would never again need approval from the Association. The fundamental prohibition against demon rum would vanish. All this relief would apply to past as well as to future buyers.

The April auction was painful – except for the speculators. Everything was for sale. The three hotels, the Pavilion, Lake Lily, hundreds of lots, seven cottages, and even the beaches were up for grabs. They all sold at a fraction of their worth. Within six short years the idealistic vision of **Alexander Whilldin** had been shattered – Cape May Point would never completely fulfill his dream of developing as "a Moral and Religious Seaside Home."

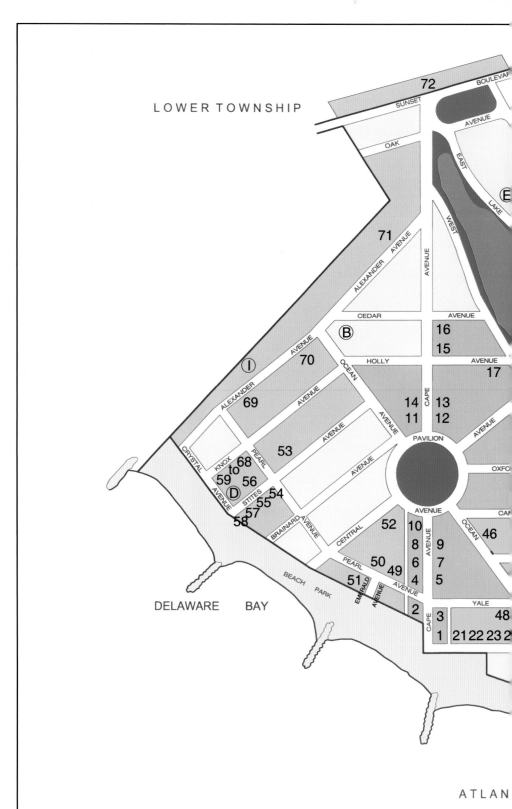

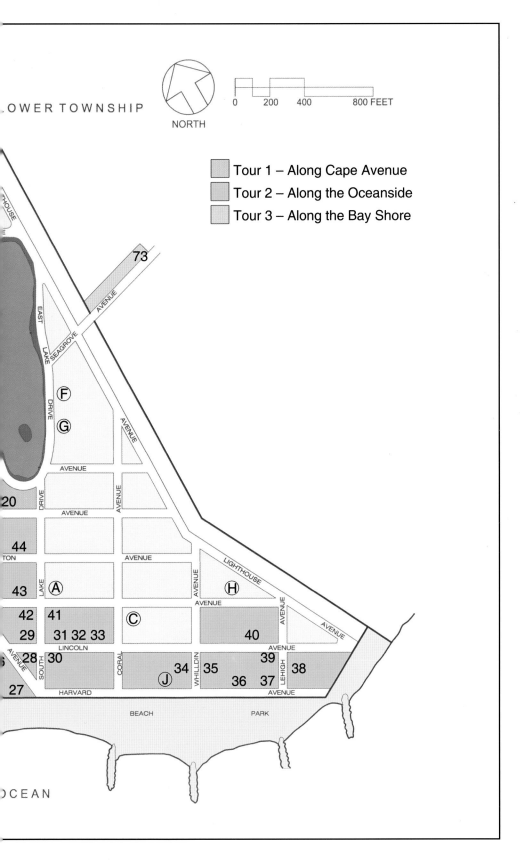

Part 2
THE SURVIVORS

I

Rev. Enock H. Supplee Cottage *c. 1877*

201 Cape Avenue

Rev. Enock H. Supplee Cottage

Obscured by a dense tangle of ivy and native plants, this remarkable *Queen Anne* cottage eludes many passersby. A tall sand berm, where a sidewalk might be expected, appears to ensure its seclusion.

This separation is regrettable, for a careful inspection reveals many delightful details. Its two-story bay, crowned with a conical hipped roof, is so prominent it seems more like an octagonal tower.

The characteristic *Queen Anne* windows, with their multiple lights of colored glass and ornamental hoods, may be found in several other Point cottages. The windows and shutters are original as are the porch posts and railings, but the siding is vinyl siding.

Built by **Smith E. Hughes,** the Germantown contractor responsible for the **Cape House Hotel** and many Point cottages, it was acquired by the **Rev. Enock H. Supplee** and his wife, **Mary,** in 1879 and remained in the Supplee family until 1944.

2
Croll-Blackburne Cottage *c. 1876*
"The Grey Ghost"
206 Cape Avenue

Everyone's favorite house in Cape May Point is undoubtedly this imposing *Victorian Gothic* cottage at the foot of Cape Avenue. Its classic picket fence and manicured landscaping were the attributes of any proper seaside cottage in the late 1800s. Its site is enviable, half in the dunes, and silhouetted at dusk against the Point's celebrated sunsets.

Croll-Blackburne Cottage

The slender cruciform plan, crowned with its steep gable roofs and enveloped in a double-decked porch painted with somber tones of gray, give it a somewhat sinister look, perhaps accounting for its familiar name: *The Grey Ghost*. Extensive repairs in 1985 copied all of the original woodwork design so the house remains little changed from its original appearance. The only new additions are the third floor decks.

This house started out on Beach Avenue next to the **Signal Station**, where commencing in 1878 **Albert Croll** amassed a half dozen contiguous lots, half of them beachfront. The house was soon moved back as erosion claimed the street, and then moved again in 1917 to its present location, the former site of the **Centennial House** Hotel, by the Croll family heirs, **Agnes Croll Blackburne** and her brother, **John Blackburne.**

Agnes and John were from a wealthy family that owned the Philadelphia block upon which **John Wanamaker** had built his famous store. Agnes summered there until 1970, when she sold the house and furniture to **George W. Qualls**, a prominent Philadelphia architect.

Fifteen years later, **Floyd W. Ohliger**, and his associate, **Ruth Tennerman Frost**, a pair interested in historic properties, bought the house and undertook extensive renovations to ensure its historic preservation. Within two years, poor health forced Ohliger to sell to the present owner, who has continued to maintain the cottage in its splendid condition.

Photo c.1910

3
George S. Fullerton Cottage *c. 1888*

Elizabeth Lownes acquired this property in 1875 from the **Sea Grove Association** with **A. W. Springer** as the builder. A disastrous fire in 1886 at the **Centennial House Hotel,** where the **Croll-Blackburne Cottage (2)** now stands, destroyed the Lownes Cottage and the house next door. Penn Professor **George S. Fullerton** bought both lots and in 1888 hired **A. W. Springer** to build this cottage. From Fullerton the house passed to **Henry E. Manges** who owned it for more than fifty years.

The perfectly square plan is surrounded on three sides by a veranda with chamfered posts and brackets carved in a tasteful *Eastlake* style. The gothic quatrefoil is repeated on the porch spandrels, along the deep eaves of the dormers, and in the unusual attic windows on all four sides. The massive hipped roof is sheathed in cement asbestos shingles laid in a diamond pattern. The staggered-butt shingles of the dormers are original, but vinyl siding now covers the old siding.

George S. Fullerton Cottage

4

Cornelius Simpson Cottage *c. 1881*

300 Cape Avenue

The corner of Cape, Pearl, and Yale Avenues was, in the nineteenth century, the commercial center of the community. Across from the Simpson Cottage, on the east corner of Cape and Yale, where the Marianist's **Wanamaker Cottage** now stands, **M. H. Golt** had opened his grocery business, with a competitor, **R. Edmonds and Son**, right next door.

Simpson soon followed the trend, offering provisions at **C. Simpson and Son** in 1881. The business was short-lived – after four years the property was sold to a Philadelphia builder, **William G. Sherrill.**

A century has gone by now and the corner is still significant – not for its stores, but for its architecture. Each of the four corners features beautiful examples of Cape May Point's historic cottages, two of them moved here, but all of them little changed from the day they were built.

The marks of the *Queen Anne* style on the upper floors are evident in the hipped roofs over the tower and the double-bay wing, in the handsome hooded windows on the upper floors, with their array of colored glass lights, and the fish scale shingles above, contrasting with the clapboard siding below.

Photo c. 1925

Cornelius Simpson Cottage

5

A style known as *American Bracketed Villa* was the preference of Sea Grove's founders **Alexander Whilldin** and **John Wanamaker** for their seaside manor houses and for the one later built for **President Benjamin H. Harrison**. Only the Wanamaker house has survived, the other two having succumbed to the ravages of the ocean.

Laever and Kneedler, contractors for the **Sea Grove House**, built it three stories high with a double-decked veranda encircling its four symmetrical sides. It remains very much the same as it was when Wanamaker opened it for Sea Grove's first season.

The very deep eaves of its shallow hipped roof hover over pairs of brackets that are clearly ornamental with no structural value. The porch post brackets of rippling scrollwork also indicate their purely decorative role. The design of the scroll-sawn balusters on the second floor is likewise restrained. The Wanamaker and Whilldin cottages set an example of modest design; the absence of ostentatious display in Cape May Point's cottage design may have been out of respect for Sea Grove's mission as a sanctuary for God-fearing middleclass gentlemen.

The Wanamaker family occupied this cottage on Beach Avenue until 1896, but three years later, as coastal storms continued to threaten it, they presented it to the Presbyterian trustees of the **Sea-Side Home**. In 1916 **Edward W. Springer** moved it to the present site where the **Presbyterian Children's Village of Philadelphia** operated it as a vacation home for the orphanage.

When foster care was replacing the need for orphanages, the Presbyterians sold the property to the **Marianist Society, Inc**. of New York, who today operate the property as a family retreat center.

Illustration c.1875

John Wanamaker Cottage

6
Floral Cottage *c. 1880*

The early days of Sea Grove saw a number of boarding houses put up to accommodate vacationers who chose to pay less than the rates for the **Sea Grove House** or for one of the rental cottages. The Floral Cottage, later changed to **Floral Villa**, was one of the first, operated by **Mary Springer** until 1919, and then by **Beulah J. Bell** as an apartment house until 1954. Much was altered over the years, especially in the 1990s when it became a three-unit condominium. A comparison with the 1890 photo shows extensive changes from the character of the original building.

Floral Cottage

Photo c.1890

26

7

Caroline G. Boughton Cottage *c. 1881*
"El Precio"

Caroline G. Boughton Cottage

One's first impression is that the Boughton Cottage is the twin of its immediate neighbor, but further study reveals that it is more quadruplet than twin. Its three sisters can be seen not only next door at 311 Cape, but across the street at 312 Cape, and around the corner at 313 Central Avenue.

They were probably all built by **Smith E. Hughes**, an owner of the **Hughes Brothers Lumber Yard** on Sunset Boulevard, as well as contractor for the **Cape House Hotel** and a number of local cottages. **Dr. J. Newton Walker** purchased the two double lots at auction from the **Sea Grove Association** in 1881. It seems likely that he then had Hughes construct the two adjacent houses for summer rentals from plans the contractor had used to build the cottages at 312 Cape and 313 Central.

27

In 1991 he conveyed the property to Caroline Boughton who twenty-four years later sold it to **Joseph G. Jungkurth**, the author's grandfather. It remains in his family today and its lineage has been the genesis of the author's previous book, *Cape May Point – The Illustrated History*.

Each of these four houses differ in minor details, but their common cruciform plan, with bold arched spandrels at the gable ends and carried on square chamfered brackets, set them apart from other houses of the period. The arched double doors of the upper and lower front porches repeat the arched gable design. That attractive feature is unique to this cottage.

8
The Elizabeth W. Theobald Cottage c. 1870
310 Cape Avenue

To classify the architectural style of this modest house as *Early Federal* may be a questionable assumption, but it clearly stands apart from the ubiquitous *Carpenter Gothic* form of most of its neighbors.

Although moved here in the mid-Forties from a choice oceanfront site beyond the **Croll-Blackburne Cottage (2)**, that was not its original location. It reportedly started life about a mile away in West Cape May, on Stevens Street next to **Rea's Farm**, and traveled to Cape May Point around 1900.

Few Point cottages have their ridgeline parallel with the street; usually it's the gable end that is featured. The two-over-two sash is more Victorian than Georgian, but it is original, as are the shutters and clapboard. This makes it one of the few houses that have not succumbed to replacement siding of vinyl or cement asbestos.

The Elizabeth W. Theobald Cottage

Jane McClellan Barr Cottage *c. 1881*
"Penpoint"
311 Cape Avenue

The Barr Cottage remains the least altered of the quadruplets. Its open wrap-around porch without railings between the posts was a common scheme for the early Sea Grove cottages. It lacks the second floor porch of its neighbor at 309 Cape (a 1915 addition when Mr. Jungkurth converted the second floor to a rental apartment).

A pair of attic windows contrasts with the single triangular sash of the house next door. Likewise, the two second-floor windows differ from the arched double doors at 309 Cape. The rococo shapes of the scroll-sawn brackets and pendants are representative of most of the fretwork found in the Point cottages of its era.

Jane McClellan Barr Cottage

10
Leaming M. Whilldin Cottage *c. 1877*

Within a year after **Smith E. Hughes** built this cottage (another of the quadruplets) it became the property of the Whilldin family. Leaming Whilldin soon passed it on to **Jane G. Whilldin**, wife of **Alexander Whilldin**. Since Jane and Alexander, the founders of Sea Grove, lived in a grand beachfront villa, it seems likely that they leased it as a summer rental during the seven years it was in their family.

Frank S. Rutherford, a realtor and builder who put up many a Point cottage over a thirty-year career, became the owner in 1923. He enlarged the porch, changing its roofline, and enclosed the northern end for his real estate office.

Like 309 Cape, the attic window is a small triangle, but unlike 311 Cape, which has two windows in the second-floor bedroom, this cottage has three. Some fretwork is missing from the front gable, and like 311 Cape, cement asbestos shingles have replaced the original clapboard.

Leaming M. Whilldin Cottage

The Cape May Point General Store c. 1940
500 Cape Avenue

Long gone are the dozens of stores that were scattered around Cape May Point in the late 1800s. This is the only remainder of the numerous shops and stores that sold everything from fish to footwear.

Frank Rutherford built the present store for **Joseph McCullough** in 1940, and for six years it was simply called **McCullough's**. Then followed a succession of proprietors and regular name changes: **Kreiger's, Kenyon's Corner, Berghaus's, Harriet's**, and finally under the present owner, **Doris Dwyer**, it became a generic **Cape May Point General Store**.

In many ways it is a nineteenth century general store – a combination toy store, soup-and-sandwich shop, convenience store, bakery, and all-around meeting place for Cape May Pointers from dawn until dusk.

The Cape May Point General Store

12
Saint Agnes Catholic Church *c. 1885*
501 Cape Avenue

Saint Agnes' stucco exterior suggests a masonry building, but it is actually a frame structure. It bears the familiar characteristics of the *Carpenter Gothic* style much favored for church design at that time.

It lacks a bell tower or steeple but the large cross atop the steep gable roof proudly announces its Roman Catholic denomination. One of its most attractive features is the array of slender gothic casement windows of brilliant leaded glass. Surprisingly, these sashes are quite new, although they are fitted into the original wood frames.

Saint Agnes Catholic Church

13

John Corson Cottage *c. 1876*

The most striking aspect of this cottage, setting it apart from its contemporaries, is its long, slender, rectangular plan capped by an unadorned gable roof. The unusual double-deck veranda is more recent, constructed shortly before the First World War. The original one-story veranda ran across the western gable end and partway down the south side.

At the very rear of the property, an old, rare, board-and-batten stable that contained the kitchen at an earlier time is still connected to the house by a covered walkway. Before 1881 the kitchen prepared food for the worshipers at the nearby **Pavilion**.

The first floor windows, which now replace the earlier French doors, extend to the porch floor with a wood panel forming a base under the sash. The shutters are old, but the siding has been replaced. Still standing, but barely so, is a picket fence that was *de rigueur* for a proper cottage of its time. Following the First World War the home was acquired by the **Crowe Family** and has remained in their possession ever since.

John Corson Cottage

14

Beadle Memorial Church *c. 1882*

Isaac Purcell, a prominent Philadelphia architect who studied with **Samuel Sloan**, designed this unique Presbyterian chapel. The unusual floor plan is remarkably different from the simple naves of the other Point churches. The Beadle Memorial, because of the stick style overlay of its exterior walls, bears a certain resemblance to another Point church, **Saint Peter's-by-the-Sea (28).**

The church's unusual name honors **Rev. Elias R. Beadle**, pastor of the First Presbyterian Church at 21st and Walnut Streets in Philadelphia. The personal connections here are interesting – Reverend Beadle was the Philadelphia pastor of the **Wanamaker** family, and a summer vacationer in Cape May Point.

Like Saint Peter's-by-the-Sea, this church has been moved from site to site. Its first home was at the corner of Diamond and Emerald Avenues, one block back from the beach. By 1920 this had become a precarious beachfront property. The church was moved to the west side of Pearl Avenue, between Emerald and Cape Avenues, and remained safely there for 45 years.

The great 1962 storm convinced the congregation that another move was worth considering. This would be more complicated than the previous one — there were many obstacles along the five-block route it would take to its current location.

The moving contractor jacked up the light frame structure and ever so slowly rolled it up Pearl to Cape, took a left on Cape, traveled halfway around Pavilion Circle, then right on Cape a few hundred feet to its new (and current) home. All went well — the church was secured to its new foundation, utility lines were restored and everybody went home. On July 3, 1966 the church was rededicated in a joyful opening service.

Beadle Memorial Church

15

The John & Linda Kelly Cottage c. 1890

In a seashore community, everyone wants to live close to the beach. Development along Cape Avenue beyond Pavilion Circle was understandably slow through the 1950s. It is reasonable, therefore, to assume that this modest Victorian cottage was moved to its present site, since its date of origin is unavailable from public records.

The simple arrangement of rectangular plan, plain gable roof, two-over-two windows (though not all are original), and el-shaped porch can be found in many other Point houses. The house originally had four rooms – two upstairs and two downstairs. The open front porch was rebuilt in 1993, with turned posts replacing the original chamfered square posts. The south portion has been enclosed and the north wing was added in 1977.

The John & Linda Kelly Cottage

16

The William & Helen McDowell Cottage c. 1890

Chances are that this little cottage, like the **Kelly Cottage (15)** down the street, had been built elsewhere and moved to this corner. Very little remains to tell us what the house was like in the beginning, but the painted clapboard and second-story front window attest to its age.

The one-story front has been added, and most of the windows changed from early double-hung to recent jalousies.

*The William & Helen
McDowell Cottage*

17
William M. Boyer Cottage *c.1877*
402 Holly Avenue

Jeremiah H. Townsend, a local master carpenter responsible for much of the early construction in Cape May Point, erected this el-shaped cottage for **William M. Boyer**, who lived there for seventeen years.

There is reason to believe that the small corner porch had previously extended across the front of the house, for this was the fashion of that period. It has retained the early windows and waveform bargeboard, but the clapboard is made of aluminum.

William M. Boyer Cottage

18
Cape May Point Social Club *c. 1899*

A physician from Pittsburgh, **Dr. Randall T. Hazzard**, converted an abandoned icehouse built by **Jeremiah Townsend** for **J. Newton Walker** in the 1870s, into *The Cape May Social Club*. With its wide porches commanding a great view of Lake Lily, and its giant parlor furnished with a dazzling fireplace and elegant stairway, it was a splendid transformation. The social club had many aliases. On any day the press might have referred to it as the *Lakeside Lodge*, *Lily Lake Casino*, or the *Lakeside Villa*.

Announcing that its object was "the advancement of social life in Cape May Point," it opened its doors on August 11, 1899 with (what else) a reception and tea. Fittingly, Dr. Hazzard became the first president.

Determined to make the lake and the clubhouse the focal point of social life, Hazzard also built the famous **Rustic Bridge** overlooking the clumps of lily pads at the north end of the lake.

Very little has changed in its century-old life. The cedar shingles are now cement asbestos, the shutters long gone, and the second floor roof-deck railing has been removed.

Photo c.1905

Cape May Point Social Club

19

Francis L. Kirkpatrick Cottage *c. 1875*
504 West Lake Drive

A daily carriage drive around Lake Lily was a way to show off one's fine livery – a statement of status. For those who missed this spectacle, the newspaper would report on the fine team that Dr. So-and-so was driving. Nevertheless, it wasn't fashionable at that time to build one's vacation home on the lakefront. The Kirkpatrick Cottage was an exception, and the family summered there from 1875 until 1897.

Like others arranged with the ridgeline parallel to the street, it places a prominent dormer front-and-center to act as a welcoming pediment. The refined bargeboard is barely noticeable, its scrollwork of circles confined near the rafter ends. The enclosed porch and vinyl siding are obviously new.

Francis L. Kirkpatrick Cottage

20
Cape May Point Schoolhouse *c.1881*
407 Cambridge Avenue

The building put up by the trustees of **Cape May County School District #28** in 1881 wasn't literally a one-room schoolhouse – it was actually a two-room schoolhouse, because it was two stories high, with grades one through four on the open first floor and grades five through eight on the second. It's doubtful that overcrowding was ever a problem – with few year-round residents there were not many children of school age. Nevertheless, classes continued until 1931, when the Consolidated School in Lower Township took over.

The school building has survived at its original location on Cambridge Avenue, a stone's throw from the lake. The most recent owner has carefully restored it from a duplex apartment to an impressive single-family residence, retaining many of the historic features.

The old painted clapboard and the little triangular attic window are still here, but the windows have been replaced. The entrance terrace is more recent – wide wooden steps and railings formerly led to the central entrance. The school bell tower over the front gable was removed some years ago.

Photo *c.1890*

Cape May Point Schoolhouse

21-25

Walker Row Cottages *c. 1877*
"The Five Sisters"
407-415 Lincoln Avenue

Dr. J. Newton Walker, an enterprising physician from Philadelphia, is credited as the developer of these five cottages known as the **Walker Row**. He invested heavily in various local real estate ventures. He saw **Sea Grove** as "The Promised Land" – not in the biblical sense, but in the mercantile sense. He was an entrepreneur in a hurry, and this was his turf. Walker Row was an early enterprise, consisting of five identical cottages on Lincoln Avenue directly across from the **Sea Grove Hotel**. Here they still stand, each somewhat altered from its original form, and known in recent years as **The Five Sisters**. Built for Walker by **Jeremiah H. Townsend**, they opened for the Point's first season.

Sea Grove's standard lot size was 50x100. Four such lots were subdivided into five, each now 40x100. They were built as speculative rental cottages until they could be sold. The first buyer, in 1876, was **Rev. Thomas Iaeger**, a Lutheran minister from Reading, Pennsylvania, who chose #407.

Iaeger's house is among the least altered of the five, so it gives us a good image of these quintuplets in their prime. Each has a pure rectangular plan, a steep gable roof with unusually deep eaves, an el-shaped porch with a second floor deck, and a bay window on the western side. Pairs of gracefully proportioned French doors with delicate arched heads lead to the deck and porch.

The fine saw-tooth bargeboard is extended back from the gable end as running trim along the eaves. This is an unusual feature that makes the roof seem to float gracefully over the house.

21 – An addition has been built over the first floor bay window. There is reason to believe that the picket fence is original – a common fashion in **Sea Grove**. The deck railing is the original style that was found on all of these cottages, and can be seen also on the **Fogg Cottage (26)**. In the 1930s Mrs. Castle opened an ice cream parlor in this house.

415 Lincoln Avenue

22 – Many of the old shutters are still evident, the acorn pinnacle and the porch post brackets are original, but the front porch has been altered and enclosed. In the 1920s there was a store in the front parlor, but it did not survive too long.

413 Lincoln Avenue

23 – The deck railing is clearly new, and the porch roof severely altered so that it loses the delicate eave line it once had.

411 Lincoln Avenue

24 – When the present owners bought the house in 1963, the porch had already been altered, obscuring the fact that it once looked just like its neighbors. The cement asbestos siding here differs from the others, all of which have switched to vinyl siding.

409 Lincoln Avenue

25 – The richly carved balusters of the deck railing echo the fine texture of the bargeboard above, but this is a recent installation. The style of the original railing can be found on number 415. The wing on the east side is a later addition.

407 Lincoln Avenue

26

Dr. Isaac S. Fogg Cottage *c. 1876*

The antique photograph reveals how little has been done to change this cottage over the years. The railroad tracks in the foreground disappeared long ago. They carried the cars of the **Delaware Bay, Cape May, and Sewells Point Railroad** that connected the Point with the **Steamboat Landing** at **Sunset Beach**. In 1892 the electric trolley took over for the steam engine and this service continued until 1916.

The most conspicuous changes to this house are the removal of the second floor deck railing, picket fence, and diminutive acroterions that adorned the peaks of the gables. The plan is in the shape of an el with a bay window at the base of the minor wing. The slender porch posts are turned, not square, with three-dimensional brackets under the porch roof. Additional decorative brackets can be found under the gable eaves. Diagonally across the street is the **Henry Keim Cottage (29)**, a twin to this one when it was built.

Dr. Fogg was a Philadelphia dentist, and the contractor was **Jeremiah H. Townsend** of Cape May. It remained in the Fogg family until 1919.

Dr. Isaac S. Fogg Cottage

Photo c. 1890

27
Elizabeth A. Fahy Cottage *c.1877*
"Floradune"
110 Ocean Avenue

This lovely cottage, nestled in the dunes and the envy of many passing vacationers on their way to **Saint Peter's Beach**, really deserves to be called a *beach house*. It exhibits a certain stateliness, probably due to its fortunate location. Original elements include the gable finial, the turned porch posts, and the French doors leading to the open veranda. This is one of the few cottages whose owners have resisted enclosing its porch with insect screens.

Elizabeth Fahy summered here for twenty-two years. The neighborhood was quite different then. Her next-door neighbor was the **Ocean House**, owned by **J. Newton Walker**. Harvard Avenue was nearby, and there were no dunes – they came along quite recently, in 1968.

Elizabeth A. Fahy Cottage

28
Saint Peters-by-the-Sea *c. 1880*

This diminutive chapel is certainly the most photographed building in Cape May Point. It sits on its little triangular plot like a crown jewel, safeguarded by a white picket fence.

The simple form, the crisp grays and whites of its stick-style architecture account for its universal appeal. It is the wealth of textures – the lace-like scrollwork of the hanging cornice, the deep chamfers of the applied timbering, the fine slats and rails on its projecting shutters, even the star-like cutouts of the foundation panels – that cause many to refer to it as *The Gingerbread Church*.

In 1875 it was reported that the officers of the **Sea Grove Association** were donating a 100 x 100-foot lot for the erection of an **Episcopal Church**, partially to correct the impression that Sea Grove was a Presbyterian resort rather than a Christian one open to all denominations.

In 1879 the possibility of building a chapel was again talked of, and it was suggested that a fine yellow pine frame for sale at the **Centennial Buildings in Philadelphia** might be made available for the purpose. The frame was purchased in Philadelphia, disassembled for shipment, and then reassembled on the lot adjacent to **Reverend W. R. Stockton's cottage**, which had been on the corner of Harvard Avenue and Lake Drive.

The completed structure was then moved to Cape Avenue just back from Beach Avenue and across from the **Sea Grove House**. It remained at this prominent location for twenty-three years. The constant assault by the sea on Beach Avenue properties made it advisable to move it to its present site. Over the years, various improvements have been made, but none have compromised the beauty of the original structure.

Although the church was not entirely completed, opening services were held on Sunday, July 25, 1880, to standing room only, with the Bishop and seven clergy in the chancel. It has remained a summer church with services held every season since that day.

Saint Peters-by-the-Sea

29
Henry Keim Cottage *c. 1876*
401 Lincoln Avenue

Surrounded by a row of young catalpa trees and a high privet hedge, this cottage is nestled among shrubs and trees indigenous to the Point. Although this is a twin of the **Isaac Fogg Cottage (26)** across the street, many fail to notice the connection because their settings are so different.

The house retains its delicate railings around the second floor deck and the tall, gothic lancet window-like doors that are the dominant feature of the gable end.

A series of eave brackets, painted a contrasting tone, call attention to the extreme depth of the eaves. On the Lake Drive façade, the gabled wing to the right is a later addition. The Keim family owned the property until 1899.

Henry Keim Cottage

30

The Daniel & Dorothea Baker Cottage c. 1895

105 South Lake Drive

Relentless erosion along the ocean side threatened this cottage, forcing its relocation to this lot around the period of the First World War. A few years later, in 1924, the rear portion was added. It has been in the present owner's family for almost sixty years.

The turned porch posts and brackets, the scroll-sawn balusters of the porch railings, and the teardrop contours of the bargeboard all say nineteenth century. The steep porch roof and the shed roof of the wide front dormer, however, are earmarks of the *Queen Anne* style. It has been included on the tour although its precise lineage remains uncertain.

The Daniel & Dorothea Baker Cottage

31

Rev. Frederick R. Mayser Cottage *c. 1876*

The association encouraged the ministry to settle in and ensure the spiritual purity of the community by offering them free lots – the only stipulation was that they build a house within a year. The ministers responded; Protestant clergy built ten percent of the first cottages. And so Sea Grove's religious foundation was assured, and the ministers profited handsomely.

Among those who took advantage of this generous offer was Rev. Frederick R. Mayser, a Lutheran minister from Lancaster, Pennsylvania. The house is rather similar to Ocean Avenue's **Fahy Cottage (27)** in its general form, but where the wrap around porch ends on either side, a one-story enclosure completes the circle around the narrow, gabled, two-story center. It is devoid of ornament except for the fanciful scrollwork and pinnacle at the gable ridge.

Rev. Frederick R. Mayser Cottage

32

Rev. Charles F. McCauley Cottage *c. 1877*
303 Lincoln Avenue

Double-tiered verandas were not commonplace among the early Point cottages. They were mostly confined to the larger houses that followed *the American Bracketed Villa* style. Today, only three others may be found: On the **Croll-Blackburne Cottage (2)**, on the **Wanamaker Cottage (5)**, and on the **McClure Cottage (47)**. We know the **Corson Cottage (13)** had its porches added in the twentieth century. On the McCauley Cottage, the verandas seem to have been recently rebuilt; while the second floor posts are identical to those on the first floor, the turned balusters appear to be of a newer design, raising doubt about the authenticity of the upper veranda.

The arched attic window, with its six-over-one sash appears to be an alteration, but the bargeboard, of a modified saw-tooth cut, and the tall pinnacle are original. On the first floor, the shuttered windows extend to the porch floor.

Rev. Charles F. McCauley Cottage

The Quakers never established a **Friends' Meeting House** in Cape May Point, but they did hold regular worship services during the summer months at the Thomas Hilliard Cottage on Beach Avenue. It was reported in the October 14, 1897 issue of the *Friend's Intelligencer,*

Photo c.1936

"On a high piece of ground overlooking the meeting of bay and ocean, stands the cottage of Thomas Hilliard, at Cape May Point, where Friends have met in summers past, and still meet to worship God."

After the death of Thomas Hilliard the cottage remained unoccupied until 1923 when the Richards family purchased it from the Hilliard family estate. The great September storm of 1936 brought the ocean to its doorstep and severely damaged a portion of the foundation. **Professor Horace C. Richards**, of the University of Pennsylvania, had it moved back two blocks to a safe haven, on lots at the corner of Coral and Lincoln Avenues that his parents had purchased from the Sea Grove Association sixty years earlier.

Tall narrow windows, clustered in pairs and triplets, and a bold square tower are distinctive features of this handsome house. The attic level windows are especially interesting – a group of three lancet windows with pointed hood moldings. The teardrop carvings of the bargeboard reverse direction near their base. Fortunately the painted clapboard has not been covered with vinyl, a fate of so many of the old houses. The plain square porch posts, with their unadorned brace brackets, seem appropriate for this old Quaker cottage. In stark contrast and of special interest is the imposing main entrance.

Thomas T. Hilliard Cottage

34

Rev. Frederick W. Vandersloot Cottage *c.1876*

It's known that **James C. Sidney**, the British architect and planner of **Sea Grove**, laid out this cottage for **Rev. Frederick Vandersloot**, a Lutheran minister from York, Pennsylvania. One must assume that there have been considerable alterations over the years, obliterating all evidence that an architect had been responsible for its design. It's true that Sidney's talents lay more in the field of land planning (he laid out the original plan for Philadelphia's celebrated **Fairmount Park**), but his design for the **Rev. Adolph Spaeth Cottage (43)** shows a much higher competence than what we see today in the Vandersloot Cottage.

William M. P. Braun, a wealthy manufacturer who owned the entire block on which this house sits, may have been responsible for many of the changes. This was, after all, his chauffeur's residence. The rear of the building became his garage, with a wooden car ramp from grade level up to the first floor.

It displays one familiar form – the square tower cloaked with a pyramidal roof. The steep porch roof suggests a replacement, since most of the early ones in the Point were almost flat. However, the plain posts with braced brackets are found on many other houses.

The off-center placement of the pair of windows on the gable end is a curious departure from the symmetry we see almost everywhere else.

Rev. Frederick W. Vandersloot Cottage

35
The Tower Cottage c.1890

The graceful concave curvature of the roofs, at both gable ends and over the striking octagonal tower, account for the emotional response many people feel for the unusual design of this *Queen Anne* cottage that some might call picturesque.

Unusual configurations include the wide span between the turned porch posts and the narrow façade with a gable end above that is twice its width. More familiar forms are the fishtail shingles at the attic level, the clapboard siding below, and the scroll-sawn balusters of the porch railing. Real cedar roof shingles found here are a rarity – most properties have asphalt or cement asbestos roof coverings.

Photo c.1895

The Tower Cottage

36

The Sea View Cottage *c. 1880*
"Brigadune"

In 1890 the area east of Coral Avenue near the lighthouse was devoid of houses. Almost overnight the construction of two key buildings changed that. One was a charming new hotel, **The Shoreham**, on the beachfront east of Lehigh Avenue; the other was the impressive cottage that **John Wanamaker** had built as a gift for **Benjamin Harrison**, the President of the United States.

Although the national press had a field day with the story about Wanamaker's fabulous gift to the Harrisons, in no time a half-dozen huge new homes clustered around these two icons, drawn there like bees to honey. This was now the fashionable end of town.

The Sea View was just across the street from the **Harrisons** and the **Hazzards** (**Randall Hazzard** had built next door to the president at the corner of Coral and Harvard Avenues to ensure his social standing). An early Sea Grove brochure informs us that the **Sea View** was a boarding house under the care of **Miss A. S. White** as the proprietor. Later it was converted into a private residence, and has recently been restored at great expense because the years of sea front exposure have not been kind to the old lady.

The Sea View Cottage. *Courtesy Don Touzeau*

Photo c.1890

37
Saint Joseph's Cottage c.1890

It started life in the 1890s as the nearest neighbor of the **Shoreham Hotel**, facing Beach Avenue at the corner of Lehigh Avenue. By the First World War this cottage prudently marched back a hundred feet and turned around to face Lehigh Avenue, since the ocean was about to chew up Beach Avenue. Its final move across Harvard Avenue to its present site probably occurred when a 1962 storm suggested that that would be a wise thing to do.

Careful sleuthing has failed to reveal the family for which it was first built, but we know that the **Sisters of Saint Joseph** bought it in 1913 to serve as a residence for the priests who offered mass for the nuns at **Saint Mary's-by-the-Sea (38)**.

It is a delightful example of the *Queen Anne* style. The gambrel roof breaks back and then extends over the second-floor porches, dipping gracefully to the edge. Deep roof eaves crown the second floor level with ornamental and artfully arranged S-curved brackets. The deeply hooded windows on the second floor repeat the slope of the gambrel roof above. The alternating spindles of the porch railing along Lehigh Avenue combine to create a horizontal pattern that contrasts with the strong verticality of most of the façade elements.

Saint Joseph's Cottage

38

Saint Mary's-by-the-Sea c. 1890

What did Philadelphia's **Fairmount Park** have to do with the establishment of **Saint Mary's-by-the-Sea** in Cape May Point as a summer retreat house for the **Sisters of Saint Joseph**? The connection is tenuous but nevertheless interesting. The story begins in 1898. The Park commissioners were interested in adding to their holdings in the upper Wissahickon Valley, and, for $20,000, the sisters agreed to transfer to the Commission part of their land at **Mount Saint Joseph** in that area.

With this windfall in hand, the next year they were able to build **Saint Joseph's Convent**, a new summer home in Sea Isle City. To their surprise, within ten years they found it inadequate to accommodate all of the sisters, for their community kept growing.

While expansion plans were being considered, they learned of the availability of the old **Shoreham Hotel** that was up for sale in Cape May Point. It could be had for $9,000 with all its furniture – far less than the cost of a new construction in Sea Isle City. The deal was closed in short order by **Father McDermott**, pastor of old **Saint Mary's Church** in Philadelphia, who negotiated the sale and provided the money. At his request it was named Saint Mary's-by-the-Sea.

What had been the ballroom of the hotel became the chapel. The addition of a statue of Mary in the courtyard and a crucifix atop the peaked roof announced its new role as a Catholic institution.

Long gone is the broad lawn that used to lie between the Shoreham Hotel and the beach. Now there is little more than a high wooden bulkhead and massive granite boulders to hold back every tide. The sisters come here to rest and to pray. Some of their prayers may be to their patron saint, Joseph, asking him to "please, please continue to save this refuge for us."

Photo c. 1895

Saint Mary's-
by-the-Sea

39

The Queen of the Sea c.1895
106 Lehigh Avenue

Although owned by the **Sisters of Saint Joseph** since 1923, and part of the convent and retreat complex of **Saint Mary's-by-the-Sea (38)**, this had been a private home built at the corner of Whilldin and Harvard Avenues just across the street from **Randall Hazzard's** oceanfront cottage. Like the **Sea View Cottage (36)**, built about the same time, it has a gambrel roof – an uncommon style in Cape May Point. On its principal façade, its proud name, *Queen of the Sea*, is emblazoned on the arched opening that led to a former balcony. A pair of three-story bay windows flanks the front of the house, and a one-story open veranda covers three sides. Only the general form of the building remains; windows, vinyl siding, porch posts, and railings are all replacements.

Queen of the Sea

40
Long Tom c.1890
107 Lincoln Avenue

Like the 155mm Howitzer (nicknamed **Long Tom**) used in the Spanish American War, this cottage was exceptionally long when it was first built. It was the home, warehouse, and shop for the developer of several of the large cottages that went up in the vicinity of the **President Harrison Cottage** a block to the south.

An early photograph from the lighthouses shows a building over a hundred feet long with only the front quarter used as dwelling space for the owner and his workers. The building materials came from New York, salvaged from old frame houses that had been torn down to make way for new brownstones. They arrived by sailboat to the Point beach and were lightered ashore and carted to *Long Tom*.

Around the turn of the century the rear storage area became a makeshift movie theater, since it was large enough to hold an audience and its windows could be darkened with shutters.

Its third incarnation was as a studio for the celebrated artist **Jean Leon Gerome Ferris** who had its back end fitted with a skylight to bring in north light. After Ferris moved his studio to his house on Lake Lily, this big room found still another function. The author remembers vividly a visit in the early 1930s to see the curious antique electric auto that **William Braun** garaged there. *Long Tom* is now a wee bit shorter, having given up its rear third to the floodwaters of a 1944 storm. The garage door with its curvilinear timbering and the wood ramp to the garage floor can still be seen on the east side.

Long Tom

41

The Elaine DeMarco Cottage c.1895

The identity of the original owner of this unusual cottage has not been found. It could have been the first owner of the lot, **Clarence A. Mulford** of Philadelphia, who purchased the lot (and thirty-eight others) from the **Sea Grove Association** in 1881. Whether the house was on the lot at that time, and had been built by the association, we have no way of knowing. Shortly thereafter, Mulford sold all these properties to **Ellwood Becker**, a real estate broker, and from thereon the trail grows cold.

The **Blevin family** owned it from 1914 until 1938, when **Ernest A. Choate**, (author of *The Dictionary of American Bird Names*) bought it, and it remains in his family today.

Surprisingly, the prominent veranda, with its unique tapered posts, was not added until after the First World War. The most striking features, however, are the four giant gabled dormers that burst through the eaves of the hipped roof, presenting a pair of arched attic windows sitting close above the second-floor bedroom windows. Also unusual are the imbricated shingles, although they can be seen on the dormers of one other house, the **George S. Fullerton Cottage (3)** at Yale and Cape Avenues.

The Elaine DeMarco Cottage

The Idlewild Cottage c. 1880
202 South Lake Drive

The name Idlewild comes from the caption on a photograph of this house that appeared in a promotional brochure of the **Shoreham Hotel**. The name of the first owner and date of construction remain undiscovered. It wasn't built here; it was moved to this location possibly around 1919 when **Richard J. Seltzer** acquired the lot in a tax sale from the borough.

A comparison with the old photograph of the *Queen Anne Style* cottage shows that not only

The Idlewild Cottage

has the open porch been partially enclosed, but also that the Victorian turned posts and brackets have become modified *Doric* style columns, and the railings are gone. Little else has changed, yet some of the *stick-style* timbering on the octagonal tower were removed when the siding was converted to vinyl clapboard.

Photo c. 1890s

43

Rev. Adolph Spaeth Cottage *c. 1876*

Rosemere was not the first name of this beautiful cottage. **Dr. Adolph Spaeth**, a Lutheran minister and theologian from Philadelphia, who had taken advantage of the offer of a free lot to ministers, had this cottage designed by **James C. Sidney** and built by **Joseph S. Russell** and called it *Roseneath*. As a young man Dr. Spaeth tutored a family member of the **Duke of Argyle** in Scotland, and the place he lived there was called Roseneath. The house remained in his family for fifty years.

The gable roof is exceedingly steep and this verticality is reinforced in the hanging forms of the bargeboards together with the pointed forms of the window head and shutters, all characteristics of the *Carpenter Gothic* style. The arched spandrels enclose a rich filigree of scrollwork, almost lacelike in its delicacy. The second-floor deck is not original, and the attractive patterned roof shingles are a recent improvement.

Rev. Adolph Spaeth Cottage

44

The Jacqueline Baldwin Cottage c.1895

403 Princeton Avenue

Like the **Frederick R. Mayser Cottage (31)** on Lincoln Avenue, this house has a very wide porch that extends along two sides, terminating in a one-story wing that continues the porch roof line on the rear and two rear sides. The wide span between the porch posts is unusual, as is the railing-like flat spandrel that almost gives the appearance of a structural beam to justify such a span. The central pointed window is set high, seeming to join the second floor with the attic space. The two tall, slender windows extending almost to the porch floor, and the bright red porch roof reinforce the composition of contrasting horizontal and vertical lines

The Jacqueline Baldwin Cottage

45

Edward W. Springer Cottage *c. 1890*

Edward W. Springer, Jr. was a conspicuous figure in the early days of Cape May Point. He built the **Springer Store (48)** around the corner on Yale Avenue that became the primary grocery store from 1895 until 1920. He became the longest serving mayor in the Point's history, holding the office a total of twenty-three years. During the same period he ran a profitable real estate business.

The Springer Cottage has undergone few changes. The fanciful attic balcony was removed, the siding is now vinyl, and imitation shutters have been added, but the cruciform plan has not received any ill-advised additions and the porch railings and posts are just as they had been when the mayor lived there.

Photo c. 1910

Edward W. Springer Cottage

46
Howard S. Jones Cottage *c. 1876*
315 Ocean Avenue

A Philadelphia lawyer, **Howard S. Jones**, purchased the first lot in 1876 from the **Sea Grove Association** followed by the adjoining lot in 1877 so that he could build this relatively large cottage for his family. It was still a Jones property until 1939, one of the longer cottage dynasties in the Point.

Because it is so devoid of ornament, save for the humble porch brackets, one might surmise that it had been much altered over time, losing the gingerbread wood carvings found on most of its neighbors, but this is not so. With such an unpretentious appearance, and a cluster of old cedar trees screening it from the street, one might pass by, oblivious to its existence.

Howard S. Jones Cottage

47
Joseph H. McClure Cottage *c.1876*
"Somewhere in Time"

Few properties in Cape May Point have undergone more physical, colorful, or ownership changes than the McClure Cottage. It stayed with the McClures for seventeen years, then, over the next twenty-three, it found itself with half a dozen new owners.

The most memorable of these were the Lutheran Deaconesses from the **Mary J. Drexel Home** in Philadelphia, who, starting in 1915, conducted a summer boarding school for girls for thirty years. The Deaconesses, who were nurses at Philadelphia's **German Hospital** (which became the **Lankenau Hospital**), enjoyed their own summer quarters at the **Lankenau Villa** on Beach Avenue, guests of **John D. Lankenau**, a wealthy banker and president of the hospital.

The unique dress of the Deaconesses – a gray habit, high white collar, and white bonnet – made them stand out in this small town that was more familiar with the black and white habits of the Catholic nuns. With their departure, the building reverted to apartments, and during the early Forties it even sported an ice cream parlor for a few years.

Today it is a condominium, having undergone a thorough remodeling in the early 1990s. Trying to ascertain the form of the original cottage is a futile exercise, since the change from single family home to boarding school to apartment building, and finally to upscale condominium, has left little evidence of its original form. We are indebted to the developer for retaining the handsome two-tiered veranda, more gracious at the upper level where the rococo brackets reach out to almost touch, tracing a gentle arch. The lower level is lofty, the upper level refined. Beautiful landscaped gardens complete with a giant grape arbor make this one of the most delightful sites to visit.

Joseph H. McClure Cottage

48
Edward W. Springer Store *c. 1895*

First it was **Springer's** and then **Gerew's** and then the **Post Office** (as it is to-day). When **Francis Gerew** took over the grocery business in 1923 it was a two-part store. On the right, where the four paneled doors still are, was the soda fountain and ice cream parlor. On the left was the grocery store. Each could be entered separately from the street, but one could pass inside from one to the other.

It remains a simple structure, unadorned but for the braced column brackets. A hitching ring on one of the porch posts reminds us of the days when a horse was tied there while the shopping was done. No zoning laws were around to keep Springer from building right out to the street, and the shelter provided on bad days is still appreciated today.

Photo c. 1900
Courtesy of Suzanne L. Benoit

Edward W. Springer Store

49

The Shaffer Cottage c.1895
"The Blue Pearl"
503 Pearl Avenue

Many old-timers in Cape May Point still refer to this parcel as **Mrs. Shaffer's Boarding House**. **Margaret E. Shaffer** and her family did provide meals and rooms to thousands of birders during the 1920s and 1930s. **David Rutherford**, who as a child delivered milk daily from his father's dairy farm on Sunset Boulevard, remembers how, at the first day's breakfast, the guests' conversation would be lively and convivial as the birders got to know each other. The following day found the same folks at each other's throats as they argued vehemently about who saw what bird and how that was impossible during that time of year, or that bird had never been spotted in this area.

Its location in the 1800s could have been called *Boarding House Alley*, surrounded as it was by a cluster of such facilities. Adjoining the Shaffer lot on Cape Avenue was the impressive **Floral Cottage (6)** and next to that **Wright's Villa**. Almost adjacent on Pearl Avenue was the **Godfrey Cottage** that had been connected to **Rev. Corwin's** large cottage on Central Avenue to create a multi-lot complex known as the **Corwin Cottages**.

No photographs have been found to reveal how it looked in the past, but old maps confirm the only significant change to the exterior has been the enclosure of the porch.

The Shaffer Cottage

50
John H. Benezet Cottage *c. 1876*
"Land's End"

Although it may be proper form to refer to this cottage by the name of its original owner, John Benezet, it's interesting that it was only his property for a year after he purchased it from the Sea Grove Association in 1876. Benezet then sold it to **Joseph G. Harvey**, the proprietor of the **Sea Grove House**.

Although quite commonly found in Cape May at that time, the Mansard roof was seldom used in Cape May Point. There is one, however, across the street in the **Hope D. Sloan Cottage (51)**.

The total enclosure of the front portion of the building hides the fact that it had been an open veranda. The shutters and cement asbestos siding are obviously new, and the windows have been replaced, so we don't know whether they were originally grouped in twos and fours, which seems unlikely for window patterns that period. The quatrefoil designs in the eaves can also be seen in the **George S. Fullerton Cottage (3)** on Cape Avenue.

John H. Benezet Cottage

51

Hope D. Sloan Cottage *c. 1879*

Two years before the Sea Grove Association went bankrupt and sold its holdings at public auction, Hope Sloan purchased this property from the Association. For fifty years she operated it as a boarding house. At some point in time the front portion of the el-shaped porch was removed, but it is one of the few old houses that has kept its wood clapboard siding. Around the mansard roof several narrow gothic windows with hood moldings indicate the space beyond is the third-floor living quarters, not the attic.

Now that decades of erosion have removed all trace of the Beach Avenue block, this cottage looks out over the dunes, where a former owner, the University of Pennsylvania architectural historian and co-author of *Cape May – Queen of the Seaside Resorts,* **George Thomas**, constructed a short wooden bridge to a spacious deck that he built over an old garage or stable that lay buried in the dunes.

Hope D. Sloan Cottage

52

James G. McQuaide Cottage *c.1877*

After all of the alterations this cottage has undergone over the years, it is scarcely recognizable as one of the four, including the **Boughton Cottage (7)**, the **Barr Cottage (9)**, and the **Whilldin Cottage (10)**, that were built from the same house plans.

The porch roof has been reframed, an enclosed porch built at the second floor, and an outside stair added; the clapboard siding has been covered with cement asbestos siding, and it lacks the bracketed arches at the gable ends.

James G. McQuaide Cottage

53

Mary J. Shepherd Cottage *c. 1877*

On either side of the Shepherd Cottage are two identical houses that a developer put up around 1980 for speculation. Its setting now appears crowded with the high privet hedge making it difficult to see from the street. Various members of the Shepherd family held possession until the 1920s when it became the property of the Reeves family from West Cape May through marriage.

The plan is el-shaped with a tower on the eastern side that has a colorful *Queen Anne* window. The wood clapboards are still evident, but in the rear sections the siding is vinyl, suggesting that these may have been later additions. Surprisingly, while the shutters are old, the windows are new. An attractive bargeboard with a pierced and scalloped profile can be seen on the front gable.

Mary J. Shepherd Cottage

54
Parson's Folly c. 1885
221 Stites Avenue

No religious group has left reminders of its former presence in Cape May Point more conspicuously than the **United Brethren in Christ.** The row of diminutive cabins still lining the south side of Knox Avenue west of Pearl are the remnants of the **camp meeting grove** they established here in 1885. They promptly set about the construction that would transform the land into a self-contained little village of tents, cabins, and communal buildings, often referred to as "the camp grounds" or as "the grove."

A dining hall for communal meals occupied two lots across the street from the grove at the northeast corner of Stites and Pearl Avenues. This building has undergone many changes before finally, in the 1980s, being remodeled into condominium apartments by **Elizabeth Parsons**, who whimsically christened it ***Parson's Folly***.

Parson's Folly

55
The Cottee Cottage c.1908
219 Stites Avenue

According to one account, no other house in Cape May Point has undergone the remarkable transformations that this one has. It has been reported that it first came into existence as an unpretentious one-story dwelling, quite possibly a leftover from the **Camp Meeting Grounds**. The first conversion enlarged it by removing the roof and constructing a second story directly over the first. What we see today is the result of a second addition to the west that doubled the previous size. Such incremental development would explain the departure from the more common practice of having the gable end face the street.

The two-over-two windows, turned porch posts, and real wood clapboard siding all suggest that most of these changes took place early on. The Cottee family disputes this account, believing that the cottage was built for them in 1908 and enlarged by them in the 1930s.

The Cottee Cottage

56
Camp Meeting Cabin c.1885

The grounds of the **camp meeting grove** established by **The United Brethren in Christ** consisted of this block – bounded by Stites, Crystal, Knox, and Pearl Avenues. This made a grove of 200 x 250-feet, which was enclosed with a picket fence. At first tiny parcels, 15 x 24-feet, had been staked out, initially for the erection of tents. The pavilion, for the all-important worship services, occupied the very center of the lot. A third of the block, that portion fronting on Pearl Avenue, had been kept open to seat those attending the pavilion service.

As in many of the other camp meeting sites, the tents were gradually replaced with pint-sized cabins. They were little more than unwinterized wooden tents. A 1917 map shows them cheek by jowl along Knox Avenue with two other clusters radiating out from the rear of the pavilion. We do not know when the camp meetings ceased or when the **Sea Grove Campmeeting Association** gave up its active management of the property.

It has been reported that, in the 1930s, Harry Dilks, then mayor of Cape May Point, purchased the entire church property from the Association. The dining hall became his residence and he moved the center cabins out along Knox and Stites Avenues on 25 x 100-foot lots. Some have little additions; others have been delightfully altered and added to, especially along Knox Avenue, making that one block strip a special feature of the Point.

Camp Meeting Cabin

57

The Walter & Eileen Lazaroff Cottage c. 1900

The general form of this house, an el-shaped plan two stories high with intersecting gable roofs and a front porch that extends back to the rear wing, is almost a standard arrangement for Cape May Point cottages built in the nineteenth century. The second-story bay window placed at the gable end, on the other hand, is seldom seen (yet found again on the **Michael and Marilyn Kelly Cottage (58)** next door).

The porch has been enclosed and the clapboard siding covered with vinyl siding. Scarcely observable from the street, the one-story rear wing has been converted into a screened porch, and open decks have been added at the roof level to take advantage of the beautiful views over the adjacent dunes.

The Walter & Eileen Lazaroff Cottage

58

The Michael and Marilyn Kelly Cottage c.1895

For many years **Dorothy Douglas**, the previous owner of this cottage (whose inclination was to defer all building maintenance as long as possible), had to deal with a constant stream of would-be buyers, asking at what price would she be willing to sell. The buyers saw it as a dilapidated wreck that could be had for a bargain price and then renovated into a proper seaside cottage with fantastic views over the dunes. Dorothy's response was always the same, "If you had all the wealth of **J. Paul Getty**, you couldn't even afford the down payment."

Dorothy was a lovable eccentric who lived alone in fantasy rooms she created with boundless imagination. Windows sparkled with stray crystals from old chandeliers, baskets of fake fruit dangled from the ceilings making passage difficult for the curious guest, and clotheslines carried hundreds of dresses from a bygone age, turning her bedroom into an open closet. Dorothy was a collector with wit and without restraint who seemed to live in a cocoon of very personal memories.

The unique one-story addition at the front is a reminder of the days when penny candy and sodas could be bought at the store **Julia A. Gruber** ran from 1924 until 1943. Others remember it as **Kenyon's Corner** when **Joseph Kenyon** became the owner in 1947. It was faithfully restored when **Michael Kelly**, a famous journalist, war correspondent, and casualty of the Persian Gulf War, purchased it from the Douglas family several years ago.

The Michael and Marilyn Kelly Cottage

They were all pretty much the same in 1885 – just puny, one-room cabins that the **Sea Grove Campmeeting Association of the United Brethren in Christ** had put together for the faithful who came there year after year for the zealous worship services. The cabins probably remained unaltered until after the First World War when some were moved and most enlarged over the following years with one-story additions.

Two basic styles are still discernable – four with a low gable roof, and six with a gable roof of a steeper pitch. Their diminutive scale and cheek-by-jowl positioning counteract their differences and unite them in a picturesque streetscape.

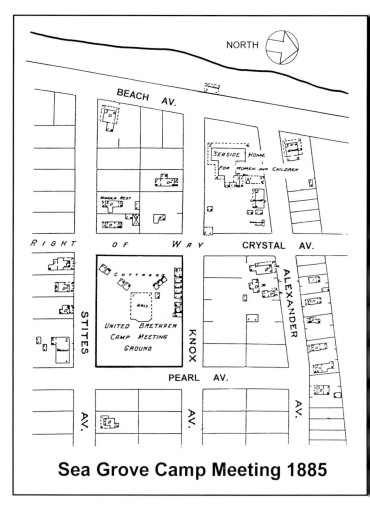

Sea Grove Camp Meeting 1885

Three owners (two of whom are architects) have created additional living space on these constricted lots by erecting two-story structures a bit behind their little cabins so that they are barely noticeable from the street. The most interesting of these is architect **Robert Cassway's Cottage (65)** where his careful attention to scale, texture, and detail, together with his wife **Esta's** exquisite gardening, make an altogether winning combination.

90

205 Knox

603 Crystal

201 Knox

207 Knox

209 Knox

211 Knox

213 Knox

92

215 Knox

217 Knox

219 Knox

69

William Y. Heberton Cottage *c. 1886*

No street in Cape May Point has experienced the changes that Alexander Avenue has. Here, far from the town center was where the maids and waiters from the hotels were to live – out of sight, and out of mind. Until World War II this was still largely a black community, where the families of those early workers continued to live.

Today Alexander Avenue has been totally rebuilt with only the **Ottinger Cottage (71)** remaining where it had been constructed. The west side is especially prized for its fine views of the Bay Shore. Its deep but narrow lots have been combined to make fifty-foot frontages.

The **William Y. Heberton Cottage** was located originally on Stites Avenue, and stayed in his family for twelve years. After a succession of owners, **Frank D. Cox II** purchased it in 1952. Erosion had brought the bay waters to its doorstep, so he had it moved here to a safe haven on Alexander Avenue.

In 2000 the present owners bought it and undertook a substantial renovation to compensate for the neglect it had endured for many years. The porch had to be re-built, so the posts and railings are new. The windows were replaced to match those that had deteriorated. Shutters, siding, and bargeboards are reproductions.

William Y. Heberton Cottage

70

The Charles & Margaret Killian Cottage c.1890
"Killian's Cape House"

At one time this cottage was the next-door neighbor of the **William Y. Heberton Cottage (69)** sitting on the northeast corner of Crystal and Stites Avenue, and it may have been moved here around the same time as Heberton's in the 1950s. The front porch has been totally remodeled and enclosed and the side porch is a recent addition. The windows have been replaced and the cedar shingles are part of the total remodeling.

Courtesy of Margaret R. Killian
Photo c.1960

The Charles & Margaret Killian Cottage

71

Lucy F. Ottinger Cottage *c. 1883*

Joseph S. Kneedler and **Justis P. Leaver** of Norristown, the Pennsylvania contractors who built the **Cape House Hotel**, erected six houses on adjacent 25-foot lots at the north end of Alexander Avenue. This cottage, the only one remaining of the original six, passed back and forth over a ten-year period between several speculators until **Lucy Ottinger** bought it in 1893. It stayed in her family until 1965.

When the present owners took possession in 1992 they knew it was in poor condition. Their assessment changed from poor to deplorable once the alterations got underway.

They found remnants of a dividing wall paralleling the ridgeline, suggesting that the house had been a two-family house, built as a 25-foot wide twin straddling two 25-foot wide lots. It still has the old cedar posts for its foundation, but much of the wood framing needed replacing.

The two-over-two Victorian windows and many of the interior doors are among the few remainders from the old cottage.

Lucy F. Ottinger Cottage

72
Wesley G. Hughes Cottage c.1875
543 Sunset Boulevard

An essential enterprise for the development of **Sea Grove** was a convenient source of lumber and building supplies for the hotels and cottages that were constantly under construction. A Philadelphia contractor, **Smith E. Hughes,** and his brother **Wesley G. Hughes** saw this opportunity and opened the first lumberyard in 1875 on the **Cape Island Turnpike** (now **Sunset Boulevard**) at the end of Cape Avenue.

The location was ideal – his materials would come in at the steamship landing (now **Sunset Beach**) and be delivered to the job site by wagon, down the Turnpike and along Cape Avenue. The **Sea Grove Lumber Yard** helped build Sea Grove. Under the management of **Wesley G. Hughes**, it provided a full line of building materials, delivering to Cape May as well as to the Point.

Next door to the lumberyard, Smith built this fine cottage for himself. Among its most interesting forms are the arched dormer windows shaded by three-sided hoods set out from the mansard roof and the four-over-four windows, which are seldom seen. More familiar are the eave brackets at the roof and post brackets at the rail-less veranda. Cement asbestos siding has replaced the older siding.

Illustration c.1878

Wesley G. Hughes Cottage

Richard Stites, Jr. House c.1772
609 Seagrove Avenue

Neither the **Wesley G. Hughes Cottage (72)** nor the **Richard Stites, Jr.** House lie in the borough of Cape May Point (they are in Lower Township), but each property made an invaluable contribution to the 1875 development of **Sea Grove**. This house, built by **Richard Stites, Jr.** in 1772 (with the easterly half added by his son, **John Stites**, around 1800) had passed through several generations when **Jane Stites Whilldin** took possession of it and 521 acres of land at the tip of the Jersey cape in 1840.

It would be another 35 years before **Alexander Whilldin** and his wife **Jane** would turn over 261 acres, the westerly half of their land, to the **Sea Grove Association** to develop the new **Sea Grove**. The Whilldins had been summering in Cape May during this period, while a nephew, **Downs Edmunds, Jr.**, had occupied the house as a tenant until 1883.

The old western half of the house has heavy timber construction and the interior shows exposed gunstock posts, summer beams, and other evidence of early *Colonial Style* framing. On the exterior all indications of the post-and-beam framing were obscured when the addition was built in the *Federal Style* at the beginning of the nineteenth century. In the late 1990s the house was listed on the **New Jersey and National Registers of Historic Places.**

Richard Stites, Jr. House

Part 3

THE DEPARTED

Two-dozen rare photographs re-evoke handsome houses that did not survive the ravages of the frequent storms that devastated one-fifth of the original community.

The Cape House
c.1880

Ocean Cottage
c.1880

Prospect Cottage
c.1890

President Harrison's Cottage
c.1895

Rustic Bridge on Lake Lily
c.1900

Overlook Cottage
c.1890

The Bungalow
c.1910

Villa Lankenau
c.1890

The Life Saving Station
c.1875

The Colonial
c.1890

Sunnyside Cottage
c.1890

The Pavilion
c. 1875

Wright's Villa and Grocery Store
c. 1915

Union Chapel
c.1900

Centennial House
c.1885

The Hughes Brothers Lumber Yard
c. 1878

The Sea-Side Home
c. 1885

Lake Lily Boathouse
c.1885

View from the Lighthouse
c.1890

The Sea Grove House
c.1875

Beach Pavilion
c. 1885

Victorian Beach House
c.1890

Sea Grove Bath Houses
c.1875

Floral Cottage
c.1900

Part 4

THE NEW ARRIVALS

A
Walter & Sally Sachs House *c.1983*
311 Yale Avenue

A paramount issue in the mind of architect **Walter Sachs** as he set out to design a home for himself and his wife, **Sally**, was *context*. He had seen that the style of many of the newer houses being built in the Point seemed out of keeping with the character of the community.

Across the street from his corner lot were two singular historic cottages, **The Elaine DeMarco Cottage (41)** and **The Idlewild Cottage (42)**. He wanted a house that would complement, but not imitate, the qualities he saw in these distinguished neighbors.

The forms, scale, and textures he employed permit the house to seem timeless – to fit in perfectly with the older houses that give Cape May Point its special flavor. He chose to use white cedar clapboards, which he had milled in South Carolina, and added no stain or preservatives. The wood has aged gracefully, except for the squirrel problem. Sally has found, to her dismay, that these hungry creatures seem to think her home is a delicious, giant acorn.

Architect – **Walter Sachs**
Construction Manager – **Kevin McCullough**

Courtesy of Sally Sachs

Walter & Sally Sachs House

115

B
Thomas & Gabrielle Larkin House *c. 2003*
401 Alexander Avenue

The basic forms here are familiar – an el-shaped plan with a simple gable roof, real wood shingles, and wraparound veranda – all reminiscent of the nineteenth-century **Sea Grove** cottages. Nevertheless, the differences are noteworthy.

Most obvious are the unique porch posts that rise up organically from the shingled railing. The placement of windows, in groups and clusters, feels just right, especially on the western gable end.

Students of architecture will notice tributes to the *Shingle Style* and the *Arts and Crafts Style,* both coincident with the *Victorian Gothic Style* that dominates the design of the early Point cottages.

The owners are both graduate architects. Their firm, **Dovetail**, has specialized in custom-designed homes, several in Cape May Point. Both collaborate on design, while Tom manages construction. His attention to detail and fine craftsmanship can be seen in the fieldstone steps and railing and in the millwork of the custom entrance door.

Architect – Gabrielle Larkin
Builder – Dovetail

Thomas & Gabrielle Larkin House

C

Don & Lorrie Touzeau House *c. 1989*
"All The Waves"
210 Yale Avenue

Two engaging design motifs are immediately evident on the Yale Avenue façade of this sophisticated beach house. The prominent entrance railing eschews the ubiquitous scroll-sawn balusters to be found on many of the Point's historic cottages in favor of undulating horizontal boards reminiscent of ocean waves.

The second unusual form is the construction of a double-gabled roof permitting a continuous ring of clerestory windows. These perform a threefold role: a decorative crown to the gable ridgeline, a brilliant light source for the upper living quarters, and from the third level loft study that overlooks the living room, a panoramic view over the surrounding rooftops to the sunsets and the sea.

We are denied a view of the spectacular façade on the opposite side, but **Lewis Tanner's** photograph tells us what we are missing. Whether the delicate but massive end columns remind us of a lighthouse or a buoy is immaterial – their association with the nearby wave railings are clearly meant to evoke, in a playful way, images of the seashore.

Though built on a standard size lot, the house appears to be larger than the allowable 2,100 square feet. It is the multiple decks with their open trellis-like roofs on either side of the gable end that create this illusion. The linear texture of trellis, railings and columns, sparkling in the sunlight, add up to a balanced symmetrical composition that is open, airy and altogether delightful.

Architect – **Thomas & Newswanger**
Builder – **Jack Hand and Sons**

Don & Lorrie Touzeau House
Photography by Lewis Tanner

Photography by Lewis Tanner

D

Randy & Janet Payne House *c.2001*
203 Knox Avenue

The original Camp Meeting Cottage on this site was in such deplorable condition that the owner, a carpenter-builder, chose to replace it with this novel two-story house. Zoning regulations restricted the total floor area to less than 800 square feet – a challenge when he needed to provide for a family of four.

The identical one-story wings on either side of the central portion contain the bedrooms – one for parents, one for the two children. Upstairs, with a spectacular view of ocean and bay through a wraparound cluster of windows, are the kitchen, dining, and living areas. Downstairs are the entrance foyer, bathrooms, and utility room.

The symmetry of the plan and window placements is not immediately apparent, but the traditional gabled roof forms, and the simple color scheme of deep green on windows and trim, contrasting sharply with the warm, light tones of the wood shingles, creates a precise and handsome composition that closely matches the scale of the old cabins around it.

Architect – Ivan Becicca
Builder – Randy Payne

Randy & Janet Payne House

E

Andrea Moffatt House *c. 2000*
711 East Lake Drive

The only hillside lots to be found in Cape May Point are along this ridge bordering the northeastern end of Lake Lily. Heavily wooded, with a magnificent old oak tree in the forefront, the landscaped areas have been confined to the steep entrance drive and the remainder left in its natural state. The use of unstained white cedar for siding and trim respects the woodland setting.

One of the most interesting features is the opening in the gable roof over the front porch. The roofline is extended to create a gable end on the street façade, while providing an open deck off the front bedroom and an enviable view of the lake.

It could have been twice its modest size because of the oversized lot, but the owner's priority was to put quality of design over quantity of house – to the delight of her architects. Like the **Payne House (D)**, the plan is essentially symmetrical about the central entrance from the driveway. This symmetry is much more apparent in the interior, where the architects have succeeded in creating a feeling of spaciousness; it is less so when viewed from Lake Drive.

***Architects* - Towers & Miller**
***Builder* – Hawthorne Davis Construction**

Courtesy of Andrea Moffatt

Andrea Moffatt House

F

J. H. Wood & B. Williams House *c. 1995*
517 East Lake Drive

Few would suspect that this comely little cottage on Lake Drive is a combination of the old and the new. Behind the screened front porch and the open deck above, an intriguing tower rises over the gable end – all of this a 1995 addition to a very modest bungalow built in the 1940s.

The miniature tower's doorway connects the deck with the newly constructed living room behind the porch. A twelve-foot expanse of sliding glass doors in the front wall of the living room ensures desirable views of the lake from parlor, porch, and deck.

The dominant expanse and refined texture of the white deck and porch railings are reminiscent of similar features on the much larger **Cupples House (G)** a few doors away.

***Designer/Builder* – Peter Savard**

J. H. Wood & B. Williams House

G

Ray and Bonnie Cupples House *c. 1995*
509 East Lake Drive

Like the old **Cape May Point Social Club (18)** on the other side of the lake, this large house stands out from its more modest neighbors when viewed from West Lake Drive. A lot almost twice the average size permitted the construction of a much larger residence.

The fashion in new construction for sites such as this that offer spectacular views over lake or ocean is what has become known as the "upside-down" house, with bedrooms on the first floor and expansive living quarters above to take in the impressive vistas. This house is an exception.

Behind the curved brow-like wall of windows is the great room, two stories high, bisected above by a bridge connecting guest rooms to the second floor deck. The owners wanted to live on the first floor, reserving second-floor bedrooms for family and friends.

The Palladian window-like entrance to the upper deck and the gable end façade is somewhat obscured, but the glistening white railings and trim define a pleasing composition of roof forms. The original owners stayed here only a few years and the new owner has added the current landscaping.

Architect – **Jack A. Thalheimer**
Builder – **Paul Burgin**

Ray and Bonnie Cupples House

H
John & Maureen Foley House c.1983
109 Yale Avenue

Whereas most of the newer houses in the Point pay homage to their older neighbors in one way or another, this one takes an uncompromising stand for "modernism."

Its careful composition of dark window openings thoughtfully arranged against its lighter skin of siding and trim is more likely to appeal to architects than to the rest of the public. It seems conceived as a piece of building art, given the highly visible sculptural contours of its spiral stair. The horizontal slots at the top of the façade imply they are openings in a railing around a roof deck, and indeed they are, affording the owners a clear view of the ocean and the evening sunsets over the bay.

The family who built this house did not retain it for long and it has passed though several owners. The identities of the architect and builder have not been found

John & Maureen Foley House

I

Ivan and Mary Becica House *c. 1998*
310 Alexander Avenue

Additions to older houses are commonplace in the Point, especially to those that started out as little bungalows. Few, however, have been so successful as this one in creating the impression that all was built at the same time.

Like the **Sachs House (A)** and the **Larkin House (B)** close by, it was designed by an architect for his own home.

By adding a shallow bay to create a gable end to the façade of the old house, he succeeded in making a seamless connection to the two-story addition to the right. The richly detailed gabled portico not only marks the entrance, but repeats the scale of that bay, reinforcing the unity of the long street façade.

Architect – Ivan Becica, AIA and Stephen Becica, AIA
Builder – Paul Burgin

Ivan and Mary Becica House

J

Robert Smith House *c. 1983*
205 Harvard Avenue

The stretch of beachfront west of Lehigh Avenue had always been the location of choice for the higher-priced homes. Expansive ocean views and southern exposure make this an ideal location. **Alexander Whilldin, John Lankenau, and President Benjamin Harrison** all had their summer homes along this section of Beach Avenue.

Following the 1962 storm, Harvard Avenue became the new "Beach Avenue," protected at last by the artificial dunes constructed in 1968.

The original owner of this house was impressed with the new home that **John Maine** had built at the corner of Harvard Avenue and Lake Drive, across from **Saint Peters-by-the-Sea**, and chose the same architect for his summer quarters.

It was one of the earlier "upside- down" schemes, placing living quarters above and minor bedrooms below. Two large oceanfront decks and a roomy interior provided the space for entertaining that the owner requested.

The low-pitched gable roof, with its delicate projecting trellis, extends far beyond the facade as if reaching out to the ocean. Large expanses of windows set in the darkened cedar siding assure that all rooms share the enviable views.

Architect - **Edward Satterthwaite**

Robert Smith House

APPENDIX

Glossary

acroterion – a carved wood ornament placed at the apex of a gable end. *See Figure 4.*

American Bracketed Villa – a popular Victorian style characterized by a square plan, symmetrical façade, low hip roof, and brackets under deep eaves. *See Figure 1.*

baluster – a small post or board supporting the top rail of a railing.

bargeboard – a carved wood board attached to the end rafters of a gable roof. *See Figure 4.*

bay – a small windowed extension to the main part of a building, usually five sided. *See Figure 3.*

berm – a wall or mound of sand or soil.

board and batten – a form of siding using wide vertical boards with thin wood strips (battens) to cover the joints between boards.

chamfered post – a beveled edge cut at a 45-degree angle; a common Victorian treatment to posts and timbering. *See Figure 2.*

clapboard siding – a common Victorian wood siding composed of long, narrow, overlapping boards with the lower edger thicker than the upper edge. *See Figures 1 and 2.*

cruciform – a cross-shaped pattern.

Doric – a classic form of round column with a simple capital.

dormer – a roofed construction projecting from a sloping roof usually housing a window known as a dormer window. *See Figure 3.*

Eastlake – a Victorian design style named for an influential English furniture designer, Charles Locke Eastlake.

eave – the lower edge of a roof projecting beyond the building's side. *See Figures 1 and 4.*

eave bracket – a decorative carved wood element placed under the eaves that is usually ornamental rather than structural. *See Figures 1 and 3.*

façade – the front of a building facing the street.

finial – the decorative top of a pinnacle.

fish scale shingles – wood shingles with a half round lower edge. *See Figures 2 and 3.*

fretwork – ornamental woodwork carved with a fret saw featuring contrasting patterns of dark and light; Victorian gingerbread. *See Figure 4.*

gable end – the triangular shaped side formed by a gable roof. *See Figure 4.*

gable roof – a double pitched roof with a ridgeline at its apex. *See Figures 3 and 4.*

gambrel roof – a double pitched roof whose slope changes between the ridgeline and the eaves.

hip roof – a roof form similar to a gable roof but with both sides and ends sloped to the eaves. *See Figure 1.*

hood molding – a projecting molding placed above the arched head of a window. *See Figure 1.*

hooded window – a window shaded by a small projecting roof supported by ornamental brackets; a common feature of the *Queen Anne* style. *See Figure 3.*

imbricated shingles – a shingle pattern with a three sided lower edge.

jalousie window – a window with overlapping slats of glass.

lancet window – a narrow window with a sharp pointed arch; often an attic window in the *Carpenter Gothic* style.

lights – the panes of glass in a window. *See Figures 2 and 3.*

pediment – a triangular gable above a window or door. *See Figure 3.*

pendant – a decorative post suspended from the apex of a gable roof's eaves and often extended through the roof ridge to form the pinnacle.

pinnacle – a decorative post mounted on the roof ridge at the gable end and often extended through to form a pendant.

post bracket – a decorative bracket, often scroll-sawn placed at the intersection of a post and beam. *See Figures 1 and 2.*

quatrefoil – a symmetrical design of four intersecting circles.

Queen Anne – a popular Victorian style characterized by an irregular floor plan, an asymmetrical façade, a complex multi-gabled roof with dormers, and exuberant use of patterns, forms, and textures. *See Figure 3.*

ridgeline - the top running edge of a gable roof. *See Figures 2 and 3.*

rococo – a style of design characterized by profuse and delicate ornamentation such as that often found in Victorian Gothic fretwork.

running trim – decorative carved wood trim with a repeated design motif. *See Figure 4.*

scroll-sawn – carved into decorative forms with a scroll saw, which has a ribbon-like blade capable of cutting curvilinear shapes. *See Figure 4.*

scroll-work – woodwork that has been cut out by a scroll saw; often called fretwork. *See Figure 4.*

spandrel –the triangular space between an arch and its rectangular enclosure. *See Figure 4.*

staggered-butt shingles – a shingle pattern formed by the alternate placing of longer and shorter length shingles next to each other in each horizontal course.

stick-style – a popular Victorian style whose principal characteristic is the application of timbering to the siding in patterns suggesting the structural framing of the building. *See Figure 2.*

timbering – the application of thicker wood boards to encase the clapboard siding of a building into a decorative series of rectangular patterns. *See Figure 2.*

turned porch posts – wood posts that have been turned on a lathe to give a round cross section with varying diameters creating a decorative silhouette. *See Figures 1 and 3.*

two-over-two sash – a double hung window with center dividers in the upper and lower sash providing two panes of glass in each. *See Figure 3.*

veranda – an open porch extending along and often around the outside of a building. *See Figures 1 and 2.*

Victorian – revived architectural style named after the period ruled by the English Queen Victoria in the late nineteenth century.

Victorian Gothic – the most common style in Cape May Point, characterized by a rectangular, el-shaped, or cruciform floor plan, steep gable roofs, scroll-sawn bargeboards, balusters, post brackets, and a prominent veranda. *See Figure 4.*

Figure 1 – American Bracketed Villa Style

1) hood molding
2) hip roof
3) eave bracket
4) eave
5) post bracket
6) clapboard siding
7) turned porch posts
8) veranda

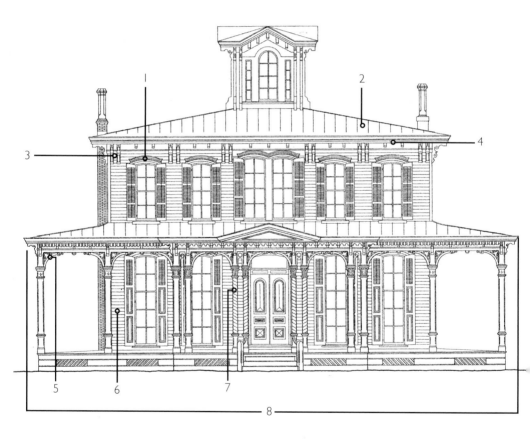

Figure 2 – Stick Style

9) ridgeline
10) hooded window
11) fish scale shingles
12) clapboard siding
13) lights
14) timbering
15) post bracket
16) chamfered post
17) veranda

137

Figure 3 – Queen Anne Style

18) dormer
19) ridgeline
20) gable roof
21) eave bracket
22) fish scale shingles
23) two-over-two sash
24) lights
25) turned porch posts
26) bay
27) pediment

Figure 4 – Victorian Gothic Style

28) gable end
29) gable roof
30) acroterion
31) bargeboard
32) eave

33) running trim
34) fretwork
35) scroll-sawn
36) scroll-work
37) spandrel

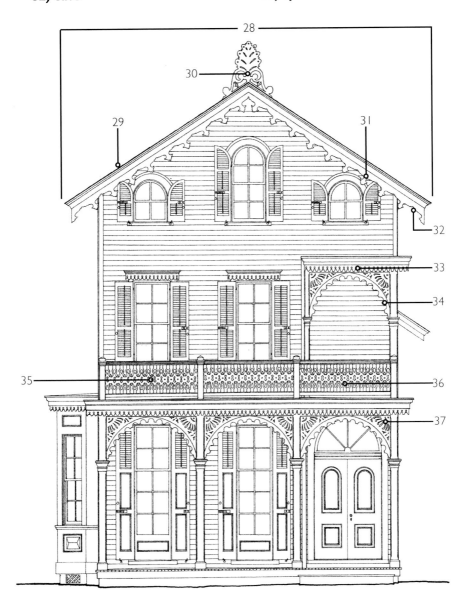

INDEX

All the Waves, 118

Baker, Daniel and Dorothea, 53
Baldwin, Jacqueline, 73
Barr, Jane McClellan, 29, 83
Barren Beach, 7
Beach Pavilion, 111
Beadle Memorial Church, 34, 35
Beadle, Rev. Elias R., 34
Becica, Ivan, AIA, 120, 130, 131
Becica, Stephen, AIA, 130
Becker, Ellwood, 70
Bell, Beulah J., 26
Benezet, John H., 81
Berghaus's, 31
Blackburne, Agnes Croll, 19
Blackburne, John, 19
Blevin Family, 70
Blue Pearl, 80
Boughton, Caroline G., 27, 83
Boyer, William M., 37
Braun, William M., 58, 69
Brigadune, 62
Bungalow, The, 104
Burgin, Paul, 126, 130

Camp Meeting Cabins, 87, 90
Camp Meeting Grounds, 86
Camp Meeting Grove, 85
Cape House, 11, 17, 27, 97, 101
Cape Island Turnpike, 8, 98
Cape May City, 6, 12
Cape May Court House, 6
Cape May Point, 7, 12
Cape May Point General Store, 31
Cape May Point School District #28, 41
Cape May Point Schoolhouse, 41
Cape May Point Social Club, 11, 38, 39,
   126

Cassway, Robert and Esta, 90
Centennial Buildings in Philadelphia, 50
Centennial House, 11,19,108
Choate, Ernest A., 70
Colonial, The, 106
Corson, John, 33, 55
Corwin Cottages, 80
Corwin, Rev. G., 80
Cottee Cottage, 86
Cox, Frank D. II, 94
Croll, Albert, 19
Croll-Blackburne Cottage, 18, 20, 28, 55
Crowe Family, 33
Cupples, Ray and Bonnie, 124, 126, 127

Delaware Bay, Cape May, and Sewells
   Point Railroad, 48
DeMarco, Elaine, 70, 114
Douglas, Dorothy, 89
Dovetail, 116
Duke of Argyle, 72
Dwyer, Doris, 31

Edmunds Jr., Downs, 100
Edmunds, R. and Son, 22
El Precio, 27
Episcopal Church, 50

Fahy, Elizabeth A., 49, 54
Fairmount Park, 58, 66
Ferris, Jean Leon Gerome, 69
Five Sisters, 42
Floradune, 49
Floral Cottage, 26, 80, 113
Floral Villa, 26
Fogg, Dr. Isaac S., 43, 48, 52
Foley, John and Maureen, 128, 129
Friends Meeting House, 56
Frost, Ruth Tannerman, 19

Fullerton, George S., 20, 21, 70, 81

Gerew, Francis, 79
Gerew's, 79
German Hospital, 77
Getty, J. Paul, 89
Gingerbread Church, 50
Godfrey Cottage, 80
Golt, M. H., 22
Gruber, Julia A., 89
Grey Ghost, 18, 19

Hand, Jack and Sons, 118
Harriet's General Store, 11, 31
Harrison, President Benjamin, 9, 24, 62, 69, 103, 132
Harvey, Joseph G., 81
Hawthorne Davis Construction, 122
Hazzard, Dr. Randolph T., 11, 38, 62, 68
Heberton, William Y., 94, 95, 96
Hilliard, Thomas T., 56, 57
Hughes Brothers Lumber Yard, 27, 109
Hughes, Smith E., 27, 30, 98
Hughes, Wesley G., 98, 99, 100

Iaeger, Rev. Thomas, 42
Idlewild Cottage, 114

Jones, Howard S., 76
Jungkurth, Joseph G., 28

Keim, Henry, 48, 52
Kelly, John and Linda, 36
Kelly, Michael and Marilyn, 88, 89
Kenyon, Joseph, 89
Kenyon's Corner, 31, 89
Killian, Charles and Margaret, 96
Killian's Cape House, 96
Kirkpatrick, Francis L., 40
Kneedler, Joseph S., 97
Kreiger's, 31

Lake Lily, 8
Lake Lily Boathouse, 110
Land's End, 81
Lankenau Hospital, 77
Lankenau, John, 77, 132
Lankenau Villa, 77
Larkin, Thomas and Gabrielle, 116, 117, 130

Lazaroff, Walter and Eileen, 88
Leaver and Kneedler, 24
Leaver, Justis P., 97
Life Saving Station, 105
Long Tom, 69
Lownes, Elizabeth, 20

Maine, John, 132
Manges, Henry E., 20
Marianist Family Retreat Center, 24
Marianist Society, Inc., 24
Mary J. Drexel Home, 77
Mayser, Rev. Frederick R., 54, 73
McCauley, Rev. Francis F., 55
McClure, Joseph H., 55, 77, 78
McCullough, Joseph, 31
McCullough, Kevin, 114
McCullough's, 31
McDermott, Father, 66
McDowell, William and Helen, 36
McQuaide, James G., 83
Moffatt, Andrea, 122, 123
Mount Saint Joseph, 66
Mrs. Shaffer's Boarding House, 80
Mulford, Clarence A., 70

National Register of Historic Places, 100
New Jersey Register of Historic Places, 100

Ocean Grove, 6
Ocean House, 49, 102
Ohliger, Floyd W., 19
Ottinger, Lucy F., 94, 97
Overlook Cottage, 104

Parson's Folly, 85
Parsons, Elizabeth, 85
Pavilion, 7, 107
Pavilion Circle, 7
Pavilion Park, 8
Payne, Randy and Janet, 120, 121, 122
Penpoint, 29
Post Office, 79
Presbyterian Children's Village of Philadelphia, 24
Prospect Cottage, 102
Purcell, Isaac, 34

Qualls, George W., FAIA, 19
Queen of the Sea, 68

Railroad Depot, 8
Rea's Farm, 28
Richards, Professor Horace C., 56
Russell, Joseph S., 72
Rustic Bridge, 12, 38, 103
Rutherford, David, 80
Rutherford, Frank S., 30, 31

Sachs, Walter and Sally, 114, 115, 130
Saint Agnes Catholic Church, 32
SaINT Joseph's Convent, 66
Saint Joseph's Cottage, 64, 65
Saint Mary's-by-the-Sea, 64, 66, 67,68
Saint Mary's Church, 66
Saint Peter's Beach, 49
Saint Peters-by-the-Sea, 34, 50, 51, 132
Satterthwaite, Edward, 132
Savard, Peter, 124
Sea Grove, 6, 42, 43, 58, 100, 116
Sea Grove Association, 6, 7, 13, 20, 27,
   50, 70, 76, 100
Sea Grove Bath Houses, 112
Sea Grove Campmeeting Association of
   the United Brethren in Christ, 87, 90
Sea Grove House, 8, 11, 24, 26, 42, 50,
   81, 111
Sea Grove Lumber Yard, 98
Sea-Side Home, 24, 109
Sea View Cottage, 62, 63, 68
Seltzer, Richard J., 71
Shaffer Cottage, 80
Shaffer, Margaret E., 80
Shepherd, Mary J., 84
Sherill, William G., 22
Shoreham Hotel, 62, 64, 66, 71
Sidney, James C., 6, 7, 72
Signal Station, 19
Simpson, C. and Son, 22, 23
Simpson, Cornelius, 22
Sisters of Saint Joseph, 64, 66, 68
Sloan, Hope D., 81, 82
Sloan, Samuel, 34
Smith, Robert, 132, 133
Somewhere in Time, 77
Spaeth, Rev. Adolph, 8, 58, 72
Springer, A. W., 20
Springer, Edward W., 24, 74, 75, 79

Springer, Mary, 26
Springer's Store, 74, 79
Steamship Landing, 8, 48
Stites, 6, 8
Stites Beach, 7
Stites, John, 100
Stites, Jr.,Richard, 100
Stockton, Rev. W. R., 9, 50
Sunnyside Cottage, 106
Sunset Beach, 48
Sunset Boulevard, 98
Supplee, Mary A., 17
Supplee, Rev. Enock H., 17

Tanner, Lewis, 118, 119
Thalheimer, Jack, 126
Theobald, Elizabeth W., 28
Thomas and Newswanger, 118
Thomas, George, 82
Touzeau, Don and Lorrie, 2, 63, 118,
   119
Tower Cottage, 60, 61
Towers and Miller, 122
Townsend, Jeremiah H., 37, 38, 42, 48

Union Chapel, 108
United Brethren in Christ, 85, 87

Vandersloot, Rev. Frederick, 58, 59
Victorian Beach House, 112
View from the Lighthouse, 110
Villa Lankenau, 105

Walker Row, 42
Walker, Dr. J. Newton, 27, 38, 42, 49
Wanamaker, John, 6, 9, 19, 22, 24, 25,
   34, 55, 62
West Cape May Land Company, 6
Whilldin, 8, 13
Whilldin, Alexander, 6, 9, 24, 30, 100,
   132
Whilldin, Jane G., 30, 100
Whilldin, Leaming M., 30, 83
White, Miss A. S., 62
Williams, B., 124, 125
Wright's Villa, 80, 107
Wood, J. H., 124, 125

Lighthouse Views: North America's Best Beacons as Captured on over 400 Postcards. Tina Skinner, Mary Martin Postcards. Just as the Victorians once traveled the shorelines in search of scenic lighthouses, collecting postcards to document their discoveries, people today react to the allure of these lights that draw tourists, collectors, and maritime fans. This book examines the postcard keepsakes that lighthouse lovers have collected since the turn of the 20th Century, documenting lighthouses from California to Alaska, and the Florida Keys to Nova Scotia. You'll see lighthouses from land, air, and sea levels in hand-tinted photographs and line drawings produced at the turn of the century, beautiful linen prints of the 1930s and '40s, and contemporary photochrome productions. Along with the images, lighthouse history and facts are conveyed, along with publishing information to help collectors identify and date their own cards. Values are shown in the captions.
Size: 8-1/2" x 11"   400 color photos 128 pp.
PriceGuide
ISBN: 0-7643-2087-4   soft cover $24.95

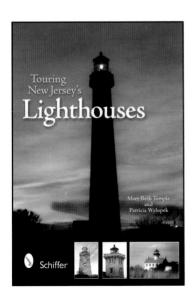

Touring New Jersey's Lighthouses. Mary Beth Temple and Patricia Wylupek. New Jersey's coastal heritage is a proud one, with lighthouses playing a starring role. This book visits eleven lighthouses accessible to the public, exploring their history as proud community sentinels and guardians of sea traffic passing treacherous rocks and shoals. From the Sandy Hook lighthouse in the north -- the nation's oldest beacon -- to popular tourist destination Cape May Point on the southern tip of the state, you can explore a great variety of styles, including the fortress-style Twin Lights, Victorian Gothic, and iron towers thrust into the sky. This is the perfect introductory tour, with a general history of lighthouses, and a thoroughly researched overview of the each light. If you have already visited some or these lights, this book will serve as a great memento. If you' have yet to discover these proud sentinels, this book will help you plan an adventure.
Size: 6" x 9"   67 images   96 pp.
ISBN: 0-7643-2093-9   soft cover $9.95

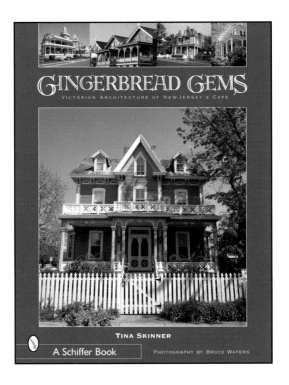

Gingerbread Gems: Victorian Architecture of Cape May. Tina Skinner & Bruce Waters. Cape May has a visual smorgasbord of Victorian architecture and ornamentation, adorned with sparkling coats of colorful paint. Gorgeous examples of Carpenter Gothic, Gothic Revival, Italianate, Second Empire, Edwardian, American Bracketed Villa, and Stick Styles are presented in color, most dating from the late 1800s to the early 1900s, and all dripping with finely cut wood bric-a-brac. Work by celebrated national architects Samuel Sloan and Frank Furness is featured, along with the area's premier local designer, Stephen Decatur Button. This picture-packed volume of summer cottages and guesthouses is a treasured souvenir for all who have visited New Jersey's southern cape, and an indispensable reference for enthusiasts of Victorian era architecture and exterior ornamentation.

Size:8 1/2" x 11"	150 color photos	80pp.
ISBN: 0-7643-1971-X	soft cover	$19.95

Schiffer books may be ordered from your local bookstore, or they may be ordered directly from the publisher by writing to:

Schiffer Publishing, Ltd.
4880 Lower Valley Rd
Atglen PA 19310
(610) 593-1777; Fax (610) 593-2002
E-mail: Info@schifferbooks.com

Please visit our web site catalog at *www.schifferbooks.com* or write for a free catalog. Please include $3.95 for shipping and handling for the first two books and $1.00 for each additional book. Free shipping for orders $100 or more.

Printed in China